Praise for *Home at Last*

"Sarada Chiruvolu writes in her Introduction, 'the individualized divinity within each of us must merge with the Absolute to experience the final destination and remain there.' For a rendition of one's 'awakening one's divinity in one's humanity and one's humanity in one's divinity' from a classical Indian perspective, I highly recommend *Home at Last* as Chiruvolu has succeeded admirably. In common language, she explicates what is inexplicable—the 'not this, not that' of what we label reality. She even alludes to what contemporary quantum physics is revealing about what the ancients long ago subscripted."

–Robert M Dittler, Ph.D., O.S.B., Abbot-Bishop, White Robed Monks of St. Benedict

"Sarada Chiruvolu's new book brilliantly takes the reader on a profound journey on the road toward enlightenment. In sharing her personal spiritual experiences in a very clear and lucid style. Sarada lights the way for us to walk the mystical path with practical feet. *Home at Last* invites us to dive deep and explore the divine waters of the ocean of bliss with Sarada as our trusted guide!"

–Dennis M. Harness, Ph.D., Vedic Astrologer and Writer

"If you are unwaveringly inclined toward spiritual discovery, especially while grounded in a "normal" family, work, and social life, you will find *Home at Last* an outpouring of wisdom, education, and guidance. Sarada Chiruvolu's *Home At Last* reveals her journey in a caring, practical way that is truthfully spoken."

–Jerry Katz, Nonduality.com

"Sarada Chiruvolu takes us into a powerful journey of self-discovery and realization. From meeting with her Guru, to her many pilgrimages to the spiritual centers of India to her deep devotion in exploring the higher realms of consciousness, *Home at Last* is a wonderful inspiration to those who are interested in finding the deep core of inner peace and consciousness. The most important aspect of Chiruvolu's path is that she remained in the world and continued her explorations without sacrificing her worldly ties. Her journey brought added light to her world and she will inspire you all to do so too. She gives us many techniques, information and knowledge of how to. Highly recommended and a must read."

–Komilla Sutton, author of *The Essential Vedic Astrology*,
President of the Komilla Academy of Vedic Sciences Inc., and
Chair of British Association of Vedic Astrology

"It has been awhile since the term Kundalini—as the touchstone of awakening and the energy behind transformation—has become an inseparable part of spiritual discourses, it is still a rare occasion when someone is able to speak from a place of direct experience and with enough clarity and authority to relate the complexity of this journey. Sarada Chiruvolu's *Home At Last* is that rare and accessible work which undoubtedly comes from most visceral encounter with this transformative power which takes the reader step by step into this extraordinary journey of Homecoming."

–Igor Kufayev, Spiritual Teacher and Meditation Master

Home at Last

Home at Last

A Journey to Higher Consciousness

SARADA CHIRUVOLU

Foreword by Amma Karunamayi

AMARYLLIS

AMARYLLIS
An imprint of Manjul Publishing House Pvt. Ltd.
• 7/32, Ansari Road, Daryaganj, New Delhi 110 002
Website: www.manjulindia.com
Registered Office:
10, Nishat Colony, Bhopal 462 003 - India
Distribution Centres:
Ahmedabad, Bengaluru, Bhopal, Kolkata, Chennai,
Hyderabad, Mumbai, New Delhi, Pune

Published by arrangement with the original publisher,
White Cloud Press.

This edition first published in 2017

ISBN 978-81-8322-660-8

Cover and Interior Degisn by C Book Services
Photos on page 75 courtesy of Sri Aurobindo Ashram Trust; photo on page 76 and at the bottom of page 77: Courtesy of Self-Realization Fellowship, Los Angles, California.

Printed and bound in India by Replika Press Private Limited

About the Author

Sarada Chiruvolu left a pharmaceutical career to pursue a spiritual calling. She set out on a unique journey that has driven her or taken her toward attaining realization of Self or Enlightenment through many years of deep meditation. Over the years since, she continues to lead a normal family life dedicating her time toward various philanthropic pursuits where ever she can make a difference. Her focus always is to address most of the rudimentary needs of people, because if these essentials are not taken care of then a detrimental cycle ensues.

She lives in Princeton, NJ. She travels extensively to other countries and annually to India to work toward this mission.

Dedication

I dedicate *Home At Last* to Sri Sri Amma Karunamayi, my teacher and guru, who has been my guiding support throughout my journey toward Enlightenment.

One hundred percent of my proceeds from *Home At Last* will be donated to SMVA Trust for Amma Karunmayi's charitable organizations.

Contents

Foreword

It was a cold and foggy winter day in December. While strong winds were blowing from the Garudaachala Mountains outside, everybody in our meditation hall was calmly mediating in dead silence. In that sublime atmosphere, I saw some kind of energy being radiated in the hall, and I wanted to discover where that wonderful light was coming from. I was amazed at the bright rays that were radiating from a lady meditating deeply close to me. That was the first time I saw Sarada deeply meditating. I started watching her through my inner vision, my third eye, as the radiance of this kind of energy, cannot be seen by the naked eye. What I saw was the bright light of an aura, which is divine in nature, like a beautiful, pure white Milky Way surrounding Sarada in deep meditation. She was encircled by that self-effulgent divine consciousness. While our inner Prana Shakti, or kundalini, can go as far as our mind can think, I could see that this bright light emanating from her could go into the universe, far beyond anybody's imagination. I could see that the Kundalini Shakti, which had been in deep slumber inside Sarada all the time, had now awakened and reached its destination.

I could see that the supreme spiritual energy, the kundalini Shakti of Sarada had blossomed and that was the reason for that grand bright light radiating around her. I could see that Sarada had attained supreme consciousness, so that now she remains in her pure self, her primal state, while fulfilling all her worldly duties. She is always aware of her own nature, the *Sat* (Ever-existent) *Chit* (Consciousness) and *Ananda* (Bliss) that is quite distinct from the body and senses but is the pure all-pervading Self, or Atman.

Sarada has transformed her life as a divine pure being through her divine thoughts, silent meditation, and service to society. Her attainment of supreme consciousness has manifested in being of service by distributing food to the poor, and giving clothing to students, supporting old age homes, and providing help in establishing water purification systems to those suffering from lack of clean water. I can see the most natural and complete inner awareness in her, whether she involves herself in social services or spiritual activities. I hope that this divine book that she has written will light the lamps in many hearts and inspire many spiritual aspirants. I wish her all the success in every endeavor.

Amma Karunamayi

Amma Karunamayi's Foreword written in her own hand in "Telugu," a dialect that is spoken in the south of India.

శ్రీ పెనుశిల క్షేత్రంలో మొట్ట మొదటిసారిగా, శారదమ్మను ధ్యాన శిబిరంలో
చూసాము. అందరూ నిశ్శబ్దంగా ధ్యానం చేస్తూ ఉన్నారు. అది
వేకువ జాము సమయము, డిసెంబరు నెల.. బయట వాతావరణం
నిండుగా పొగ మంచుతో నిండి యున్నది. విపరీతమైన చలి
చలికి వృక్షాలు వణుకుతున్నాయి. గురుదాసుల పరివారాలు సాక్షి భూతం
గా వీక్షిస్తుండగా, ఆ ఋషి భూమిలో అందరూ ధ్యానంలో ఉన్నారు

ఆ నిశ్శబ్దం అద్భుతం, పరమాద్భుతం. నిశ్శబ్దమే దైవం.

అలాంటి నిశ్చల పవిత్ర వాతావరణంలో, నాకు సమీపంలో
ధ్యానం చేస్తున్న ఒక మహిళను బాగ గమనించాను. ఎందువల్ల
అనగా, ఒక విశిష్టమైన గుండ్రని వర్తులము వంటి ఆకారమైన
వెలుగు ఆమె చుట్టూ గోచరించింది. ఇంత మహాద్భుత వెలుగు ప్రవాహం
ఎక్కడి నుండి ఉద్భవించినది, ఈ శక్తి ప్రవాహము ఏమిటి? అది
చూసాను?! ఇది అద్భుతమైన దివ్య శక్తి; ఎంతో అలౌకికమైనది.
ఈ శక్తి యొక్క తేజః సంపన్నతలో, శారదమ్మ చుట్టూ కాంతి
వలయాలు నిండి యున్నవి. అవినాశి అయిన ఈ కాంతిని
నేను నా అంతరంగ నేత్రంతో చూస్తున్నాను. ఈ కాంతి బాహ్య
నేత్రాలకి గోచరించదు.

ధ్యానం చేస్తున్న శారదమ్మ చుట్టూ
ఉత్పన్నమైన ఈ వెలుగు, పాలవంటి తెల్లని స్వచ్ఛమైన
గుండ్రని కాంతిని కలిగి యున్నది. భావన ఎంత వరకు
వెళ్ళగలదో, అంత వరకూ ప్రాణ శక్తి వెళ్ళగలదు. కాని ఈ
కాంతి భావాతీతమైన వస్తువు, ఈ వెలుగు నిఖిల బ్రహ్మాం
డమంతయు పరిభ్రమించగలదు. గాఢ నిద్రలో ఉన్న
కుండలిని శక్తి, శారదమ్మ శరీరంలో మేల్కొంటున్నది.
శారదమ్మ అంతఃస్థిత న విశ్రాంతం చెందినదని గ్రహించాము.
అదియు ఆమె శరీరం చుట్టూ అతి పెద్ద కాంతి వలయంగా
నిలచి యున్నదని గ్రహించాను.

బాహ్య ప్రపంచంలో ఉన్నా; తన అంతరంగ ప్రపంచంలో
ఉన్నా, సహజాత సహజమైన పరిణతి ఆత్మ జ్ఞానం
శారదమ్మలో నిత్యం అంతర్వాహిని.
తాను ఆత్మ అనే జ్ఞానము; శరీరము తాను కాదు
అనే సహజ జ్ఞానం నిరంతరం పడుగు, పేకల్లా
శారదమ్మలో ఉన్నది.
విరక్తి, వైరాగ్య, సాంస్కృతిక, సామా
జిక రంగాలలో, ఎంతో మందికి, శారదమ్మ అందిస్తున్న
సేవలు అనన్యమైనవి. విద్యార్థులు, నిత్యాన్నదానాలు,
దళితులకు
వస్త్రసేవలు, వృద్ధులకు పునరావాసాలు, తాగునీటి సేవలు
గుక్కెడు నీటికి నోచుకోని వారికి,
అందిస్తూ నిరుపేదల కళ్ళలో కాంతులు నింపుతుంటారు.
"బిందువు" వంటి మానవ జీవితమును, నిశ్శబ్దమైన
అంతర్మథనంతో తాను "చైతన్య సింధువు" అని
ఆత్మను ఖ్యాతి నొందిన శారదమ్మ రచించిన గ్రంథం
భక్తుల పాలిట ఆత్మజ్ఞాన కల్పవృక్షం కావాలని ఆశిస్తూ
అనేక మంగళా శాసనములతో.

ఆత్మీయకుటుంబము.

హార్‌హాట్‌వేస్ కుటుంబము విజయనగరం.

Acknowledgments

I gratefully acknowledge and thank the following people for all their support:

First, to Peter Occhiogrosso, my most diligent editor, I would like to express my deep appreciation and special thanks for all his superlative editing skills and knowledgeable input throughout my writing from beginning to end. It was a great pleasure to work with someone who is not only a skillful editor and writer, but who also has intimate knowledge of the spiritual world and its literature.

I would like to thank my beloved husband, Prem Chiruvolu, for his patience, understanding, and all his support in everything I do.

I thank my daughters, Rekha and Renu, for their input at the beginning of my writing, and my special thanks to Renu for her helpful feedback and proofreading during my initial writing of the manuscript.

I would also like to thank Steve Scholl, the Publisher of White Cloud Press for publishing my manuscript and bringing it out into the world; and Christy Collins for her sensitive help in designing my manuscript and preparing it for publication.

Finally, I would like to express my unbounded gratitude to the supreme power that is within. It has given me such inspiration and strength and has orchestrated the entire process of writing this book so that it would be possible for me to complete it.

Introduction

Enlightenment

Self-Realization

Truth

Oneness

Nondual State

Cosmic Consciousness

All these names for a state of higher consciousness have the same meaning and indicate an experience that any one of us can undergo. Don't let the spiritual terminology flabbergast you. It is not something unthinkable or unreachable or experienced only by those who leave their homes to reside in ashrams, monasteries, or caves. It is very much within everyone's reach. The speed and ease with which this transformation happens varies with each of us because it all depends on where we are in our evolutionary growth.

Home At Last explains all the intricate details and various stages I passed through over the years of this experience. But I would also like to explain that the process of realization has many layers. As the Buddhist writer Fred H. Myer, MD, writes, "Realization and Enlightenment refer to the same level of insight, but the two terms are not synonymous. . . . [R]ealization does not become enlightenment until the mind never strays from what it has realized."[1] For this to take place one must go *beyond* realization of the Self. The individualized divinity within each of us must merge with the Absolute to experience the final destination and remain there.

The purpose of the book is to delineate the Truth pertaining to the spiritual dimension of life as I have experienced it. Although it has been said by many that the realization of higher consciousness—so-called mystical experience—is much the same no matter one's religious or cultural background, each experience differs in its details. Many people have the idea that this mystical experience or discovery of our true nature is unfailingly uplifting, full of blissful moments and extraordinary visions. What I have tried to recreate in this book are the precise details of the experience, from extraordinary states of consciousness that left me feeling dazzled, to routine, everyday activities. Many books about Self-realization inspire people, but I am not aware of any that actually clarify what one goes through on the path, step by step, or give a simple description of the path to realization in the life of an otherwise ordinary individual. Most people who are curious about the mystical life need valid information along with some proof; reliable information can come only from those who have realized the information, feel it within the heart, and perceive it thoroughly through direct experience. And so that is the kind of information I have set out to provide, because I believe it can be of use to some advanced seekers while stimulating the curiosity of the general public. I feel the need is continually growing for books that can describe the path to spiritual fulfillment.

Home At Last also explains how it is possible to integrate realization into everyday life, and addresses the complex issues created by the influx of inner energy that occurs when one undergoes an active awakening. Though this inner energy can sometimes be released spontaneously, it most often requires a lengthy process of conscious practice, focusing mainly on intensive meditation. My purpose is primarily to let readers know what they can expect when confronting this mysterious, awakened inner force and how to cope with the often-harrowing physical and psychological effects of changes in consciousness they may face along the way. Our outlook and goals change radically when we are directed by the awakened inner energy rather than by our normal egoic self. Ultimately this book describes how the enlightened consciousness navigates one's given life and integrates that life with higher consciousness after attaining realization.

This is not a "how to" book in the conventional sense, mainly because the path to enlightenment can't be laid out like the directions in a cookbook, step by step with exact measurements. Even if the endpoint tends to be the same for everyone, what individuals experience on their journeys can differ quite a bit. However, the book does provide essential signposts of progress based on my own direct experience, explained in each chapter. I believe that what readers need more than ever are role models and road maps for navigating their own journeys. This guidance can be useful to anyone who may be contemplating the pursuit of higher consciousness or who simply wants to learn more about it.

Each detail is important in its own way, because we live in a material world and yet our highest calling is to a state of nonduality, or oneness, that both transcends the material and incorporates it. If that statement sounds somewhat mystifying, I hope to be able to make it clear in the pages that follow.

ONE
An Experience of Bliss

On a hot summer's day I was sitting under my favorite meditation tree in my back yard in Princeton, New Jersey. I was comfortable on my familiar bamboo stool like those used in India, because I've never enjoyed twisting myself into the so-called lotus position, cross-legged on a bare floor, during long hours of meditation. Indeed, I disliked meditating on a floor at all, preferring to sit outdoors as often as possible, even in the chill New Jersey winters, because of my intense connection with nature, which extends back as far as I can remember, into early childhood. Being in nature always helps me gain entry to a state of relaxed tranquility, at one with sun and sky, grass and trees. Usually it's cool enough in my yard during summer, but on this particular day it was excruciatingly hot—at least ninety degrees, with very high humidity. Such intense humidity can be so unpleasant that it's nearly impossible to carry on outdoor activities, although I'm not sure that meditation qualifies as an "activity."

Although I had been debating whether or not to stay indoors on such a blistering day, I finally chose to go outside, under my tree, despite the uncomfortable weather. And no sooner had I sat down that I felt a cool breeze passing through the yard, which continued to blow over me during my entire meditation. This puzzled me, because I could not see even one leaf or branch moving on any of the surrounding trees or bushes, which remained as still as could be. Even as I sank into my quietude, I could not tell where that breeze came from, but I was feeling blessed and happy on my small bamboo stool.

Sarada's back yard where she meditated with deer visitors

My daily meditations had been progressing rapidly, to the point where I could now feel surplus energy rushing through my body and being drawn upward by the equivalent of a powerful magnet. When this had started happening a few weeks prior, I was rendered so absolutely still that I felt as though I'd been incapacitated. As I had entered into a deeper realm of consciousness than ever before, I experienced a heaviness that was different from my earlier meditative states. The heaviness in my head signaled that the vital energy of my entire system was finally reaching its destination at the crown chakra. The ancient Sanskrit name of this energy center means "thousand-petaled," describing the multicolored fountains of light said to shoot from the cranium at the moment the inner energy completes its long journey upward from the base of the spine.

Today, as I continued sitting, I felt like a conscious spectator watching the flow of energy, my awareness increasing and expanding exponentially in all directions. My normal field of vision disappeared, and yet everything looked as clear as if I were seeing through what we call the "third eye," between the two brows. I felt an intense vibration and steady pressure, and my mind became quiet—but not through any effort of mine. Instead, "it" quieted itself and moved to a different dimension all on its own, and I felt as though I were in a plane that was being flown on automatic pilot. The subjective stillness I experienced was aware of itself and alive, yet without any conscious thoughts that I could verbalize. In a sense, my mind—by which I mean the accustomed flow of cognitive, rational processes—no longer existed as I had known it. It had simply stepped back and was playing no role beyond observing and understanding wordlessly.

Along with a new, deeper sense of clarity and focus, I felt a distinct relaxation of the whole system; something inside had finally freed itself from carrying a heavy burden and was being released. In that moment the realization came that I am not my body, that I am never actually *in* the body, and that what I was calling the body was merely the densest form of materialized consciousness. I could perceive it as nothingness, emptiness, void, or infinite space—names that I had read often but until now had never really comprehended.

After some time in this state I experienced a profound sense of quiet and stability, as if a huge storm had at last calmed down. The internal visual field I perceived when my eyes were closed looked soothing, like the sky at dusk. Immediately after this, the clear light of a bright golden sphere displayed itself surrounding a smaller, opal-blue sphere, each sphere appearing in sequence. This double sphere of light did not remain fixed at first, but seemed to waver. With continued meditation practice in the months to come, it would last longer and its clarity would become sharper, the distinct bright gold encircling a glorious dark blue sphere. But even at this early stage I had no doubt that the spheres represented our inner Divinity revealing itself to me.

I had read that meditation properly done tends to compel a normally silent region in the brain into an astonishing level of activity, which galvanizes the nervous system like an electric current. The result is said to be something that we can never experience in ordinary consciousness, and surely the vision I was having was so full of life that I couldn't compare it to any visual experience from the past. As I focused more and more intently and my concentration grew deeper, the light disappeared and immediately the unmistakable color of the sky at dusk spread in all directions. This back-and-forth fluctuation went on until the field became homogeneous and I felt as if I were staring at the sky itself—as though I had merged into this expansion of energy, as though we were all nothing *but* energy. I had become completely submerged in the natural, primordial state, in which I was sure of the Divinity and felt the presence of universal consciousness appearing as one continuous spectrum.

At that point I recalled the Tibetan Buddhist view that consciousness is composed of multiple shades, bands, or levels—not separate layers but more like mutually interpenetrating forms of energy, from the finest all-radiating, all-pervading, luminous consciousness down to the densest form of materialized awareness, which appears to us as our physical body. Once we reach this higher field, nothing disturbs it. Obstacles or outside forces of nature such as wind, rain, heat, and snow do not have any impact on the field, and it remains calm and unchanging. The deep inner peace and tranquility that results is not affected after we have entered the void, and so I felt I could stay there for any length of time, liberated from the bondage of my outer form. The freedom and peace that emanated from this dimension made me indifferent to my own body and sense organs. Once I achieved this state of utter stillness, absolutely nothing bothered me.

And so, throughout several hours in the ninety-degree heat and high humidity, I remained comfortable the whole time. At the end of my meditation, I felt refreshed and looked down to see not even a drop of sweat anywhere on my body or clothing. I thanked the Divine for creating the breeze that seemed to keep me cool and refreshed under my tree, even though I still could not see a single leaf in the adjoining trees move in the air. I thanked the tree that I sat under, because I believe that when we are in tune with nature, it helps us whenever we need help. It is simply a matter of believing that we are all one.

After being immersed in the peace and energy of utmost silence for a long time, I stood, picked up my bamboo stool, and returned to the noisy outer life in which I continued to play my given role. Walking back into my home, I grabbed a few oranges to squeeze for my daily fresh juice and a ripe banana from the kitchen table—the first things I feed my system to start the day. But on this day, after drinking my juice and as I was still eating the banana, I was suddenly transported back to a time when I was six years old and living with my parents in a small town in India near New Delhi.

I saw a small girl sitting on the front fender of a bicycle (the only form of transportation there) pedaled by her father. He picked her up every day from a nearby English medium school, a private Catholic school run by nuns and the only school where English was taught. The students came from different religious backgrounds, and so the nuns emphasized English rather than Catholicism in their teaching. Every day the girl's father dropped her off and picked her up from the school on his bicycle, and as he was pedaling home, the first thing she would ask was whether she could have a banana from one of the many small stores along the way. Bananas were her favorite treat, and the variety was astonishing, so she immensely enjoyed choosing a different type each day during her ride home. The wide diversity of bananas may seem odd to anyone who has grown up in the West, especially in North America and Europe, which are usually limited to the yellow and occasionally red varieties, which all taste pretty much the same. But in India bananas were available with different textures to both the skin and the flesh, and great variation in the thickness of the peel itself. Some of the smaller bananas had skins resembling those of onions; some tasted sweeter than others and had a unique flavor. So perhaps it wasn't so strange that the girl always asked for a banana instead of the other snacks that were available from the shops along the way; fruits had always been her favorite food anyway. It was such a simple request that no father could say no, and he stopped each day to buy a few bananas from a shop and give one to his daughter.

This book is about that little girl who loved bananas and enjoyed the simple routine life she led in India until she came to the United States to rejoin her parents, who had moved here before her. It is also about the inner journey that eventually brings us all to the ultimate understanding of life and its purpose. *Home At Last* explains in plain language how an average individual can reach the ultimate state of union with all of life. That union is the purpose and the ultimate goal of human existence. We are all in the same boat; it is as simple as that.

Some readers may feel that the account with which this chapter began describes an extraordinary state of consciousness that they would never be able to achieve. Yet I urge you not to stop here. Reaching higher states of consciousness is a long process that does require a strong commitment, but anything is possible when you persist, and it is definitely worth the effort. After more than nine years of practicing, I have come to believe that intensive meditation is the truest path to realization or enlightenment. However, my purpose in writing this book is to show that anyone who is ready and has reached a certain point in his or her evolutionary growth certainly has the potential to open the door toward higher states of consciousness.

As I say this, I'm aware that some people may question my remarks, insisting that other paths can also be effective. I would agree, although I do feel that meditation is the most direct path to Self-realization. Other routes, such as the path of love for and devotion to God, known as bhakti yoga, or the way to God through selfless actions and service, called karma yoga, will eventually bring you to realization. Yet I believe that those paths will take much longer, perhaps many lifetimes, before one can experience enlightenment. When I discuss meditation in more depth in a subsequent chapter, I will note that all the world's great spiritual masters practiced some form of meditation, whether or not they taught it explicitly to their followers. And it is likely that the meditation derived from traditions such as Buddhism, Christianity, Sufism, and Kabbalah also lead to realization. But because I have not practiced those traditions I can't speak from that experience. I can speak only about the form and method of meditation that I have practiced that brought me to my own realization.

One thing I believe without question is that by wholeheartedly implementing some simple guidelines in your daily life, you will greatly increase your progress on your spiritual journey. Everything I describe throughout this book I have practiced meticulously during my own journey, and each of these principles and techniques became habit-forming over time. The guidelines I'll provide below will help you build the awareness and stamina you need to reach higher states while maintaining a daily life that may consist of holding a job or practicing a profession, raising a family, and struggling through all the normal trials of life that most people endure.

After you implement these easy, effective guidelines, which have been practiced by many great sages and saints, your meditations will progress and you will be able to shift your consciousness to higher levels. This in turn will lead to more subtle perceptions and help you achieve physical, mental, and emotional harmony.

Simple Tips for Your Progress

1. Keep your body clean and healthy by nourishing it with proper food and exercise. For most people this means eating less meat and more fruits and vegetables, and consuming more liquids, especially water. This way you will expend less energy in digestion, which will help you conserve your inner energy for the goal you have set out to accomplish.
2. Get restful sleep that will allow your body to heal itself of any ailments and leave you refreshed, with plenty of energy for the

spiritual work ahead of you. Sufficient sleep is just as important as proper food and exercise as your system becomes rejuvenated.

3. Try to spend more time with outdoor activities so that you are exposed to sun daily. This is the best way to keep your body supplied with essential vitamin D, as well as the cosmic energy that the sun provides.

4. Decrease inessential activities and overall busyness. You may need to carry out the household chores associated with raising a family, as well as the work associated with your job, but you can cut down on unnecessary time spent watching TV, surfing the Web, sending e-mail, and engaging in other electronic activities. Some of these may be essential for your work, but it's surprising how many hours we spend with inessential entertainment.

5. Involve yourself with some kind of spiritual activity daily, such as reading spiritual books or scriptures, doing yoga, praying, listening to spiritual discourses, and even attending retreats and spiritual workshops. This will open the door toward the higher dimension of your consciousness.

6. Complete all your daily tasks prior to meditation. Do not give your mind a chance to be distracted by all the tasks that still need to be done.

7. Create a location to sit quietly each day even if only for a few minutes. It is preferable to meditate at the *same time and in the same place* each day, which allows you to increase the amount of time you can spend sitting in meditation. Some people meditate for a few minutes when they first wake up and again just before they go to sleep at night.

8. Increase your vital energy, also called *prana*, by doing deep breathing at least five minutes before starting to meditate. This calms the mind and prepares the way for meditation. (I'll give detailed guidance on deep breathing techniques in a subsequent chapter.)

9. Find a guru or a teacher who resonates with you, and stick to that one without constantly shopping around. Use the tools your teacher gives you on a steady basis.

10. Never let yourself get disappointed or frustrated with your efforts to the extent that you want to give up. Be patient and understand that the process will take time and can't be achieved overnight.

In following all the tips I have just laid out for you, focus above all on your desire to know the Truth. The intensity of your longing for divine union is the propelling force that will move you forward. I cannot emphasize enough how determined I was to continue my daily meditations despite the difficulties. Such determination will help you move forward more rapidly on your path.

TWO
Reiki Healing

In my exploration of holistic and complementary healing methods, I was especially drawn to Reiki, a form of touch healing that was created over a century ago by a Japanese Buddhist and has been practiced increasingly in the West. I made a decision to study Reiki first by reading every book I could find on the subject and then by receiving initiation from a Reiki master, followed by periods of practice. In time I learned Reiki healing and became certified to practice healing others.

Reiki, whose name means "Universal Life Energy," is a higher energy that can be channeled through the practitioner's body and focused on an object for the purpose of healing. The vital energy that pulsates and flows in all living things is what causes us to be alive. When this "life force energy" is depleted or suffers an imbalance, we are more likely to get sick or feel stress; when it is high, we are more capable of being healthy. Reiki is also the name applied to a healing technique that utilizes this universal life force to heal the body at all levels (physical, mental, emotional, and spiritual) by allowing us to absorb more of this energy from the universe. The process amounts to taking energy from the universal energy bank that is the source of all creation. The energy flows into us through the crown chakra, the energy center at the top of the head, and flows out through our hands to the person in need of healing. In the process it opens and expands the capacity of the body's central power channel to transmit *ki* (the life energy also known as *prana* or *chi*) and clears other channels of energy obstructions. It is similar to the healing method that was used by Christ and the Buddha.

More than anything, though, Reiki is a harmonizing energy that balances out any imbalances within the system. It works with the principles of intention and focus and can be beneficial not only to humans but to plants, animals, or any living beings. The key to Reiki healing is the application of certain pictorial characters and names as symbols, along with mantras that were derived from Sanskrit sutras, or teachings. It is known that these symbols and mantras cause our inner channels to increase their vibrational frequency in order to transfer more energy to the recipient. To do this, one has to get "energy attunements," the equivalent of being initiated or receiving transmissions of energy to practice healing. The purpose of these attunements, which I received from my Reiki master, is primarily to release blocks or toxins from our inner channels. This allows the life force energy to flow through us more intensely while our body is adjusting to the higher energy vibration that we are encountering. There are three levels of attunements, each of which gives you more knowledge and experience in healing. Each attunement increases the vibrational frequency of our chakras, or inner centers of psychophysical energy, opening the physical body to take in more universal life energy. These attunements also create a heightened amount of pranic energy, which may awaken the dormant inner energy, or kundalini, as the main channels and chakras are cleared from blockages. Clearing the channels and chakras allows us to take more universal energy into our system and helps promote healing. Yet it's unlikely to lead to any kind of spontaneous enlightenment, at least until we integrate the mind, body, and spirit. This is possible only when we bring the inner energy upward from the root chakra at the base of the spine to the crown of the head. Simply awakening the inner energy will not lead to realization, because for the individualized soul to reunite with the Source requires a lengthy process of deep meditation.

By no means is Reiki a substitute for treatment by conventional Western medicine, but it supports the natural healing process. In the years since I was initiated into Reiki healing, I have been supported by my faith in its ability to heal; both the practitioner and the recipient should believe that this kind of healing will work. At the same time, I have felt the heat and vibration of that energy directly in my head and especially in my hands, experiencing a tingling sensation while I was healing, as well as while I was meditating.

The principles of Reiki are consistent with those of yoga, which are based on the existence of invisible nerve channels in our subtle body (the subtle, or etheric, body interpenetrates the physical body). The most important nerve channel in the subtle body is the *sushumna*, which runs through the spinal column, from the base of the spine to the crown of the head, encompassing the seven concentrated life energy centers in the spine and brain called the chakras. Each chakra corresponds to a set of nerve ganglia and certain internal organs, as I will explain in more detail in chapter 10. The knowledge and understanding of these chakras is essential for both Reiki healing and Self-realization.

Being initiated by a Reiki master began a process of cleansing the chakras that I believe set the stage for the meditation that I later undertook. Although I practiced Reiki on myself, after a time the need arose to use it to help my husband, who had had what the doctors later called a symptomless heart attack. Because his situation had been ignored, part of his heart muscle was damaged. Other complications prompted him to seek medical attention, and he was eventually referred to a cardiologist, who performed a quadruple bypass operation. Though the immediate danger was rectified for the time being, his heart muscle had lost pumping capability and was no longer functioning as before. What they call an "ejection factor"—which measures the amount of blood pumped through the heart to the rest of the body—had been reduced tremendously. This is when I stepped in and performed Reiki diligently on his heart muscle, with the intention of providing more pranic energy for it to regain some of its capacity and stability and to enhance its natural healing capability. I also used Reiki to alleviate his postoperative discomfort and help him regain his strength.

I am not saying that Reiki can clear arterial blockages that lead to heart attacks or prevent future attacks, but it does improve the patient's overall condition. I had such confidence and faith in the Divine that I knew it would help my husband heal faster. After I had been practicing Reiki for some time, I began to feel a kind of sadness whenever I saw anyone suffering pain or discomfort, especially those to whom I felt close. In retrospect, I believe that on some level practicing Reiki increased my feeling of compassion for those in pain; at the same time an inner spiritual change toward deeper consciousness helped me develop capacities or tools, given by the Divine, to be used to alleviate the suffering of other living creatures. And so, practicing Reiki had surprising benefits for my own life, initiating changes I could barely have expected, quite apart from helping relieve my husband's pain.

I can think of two incidents in particular that were revealing. The first occurred when I was in India with my husband. I was taking a walk by myself and noticed a group of children who were gathered around, staring at something on the ground and making all sorts of noise. I stopped and wanted to know what was going on. I noticed a bird lying helpless, shaking a bit but still alive, in the middle of the street. The children were contemplating what to do, trying to step on it and push it out of the road. I told them to stop doing that and, using a leaf as a kind of sling, I picked up the bird and took it to an area that was more secluded and had less traffic. I placed the bird in the middle of some bushes as I performed Reiki, and I decided to stay with it until it stopped shaking and I felt it was resting. I was so involved in making sure it was okay that I had forgotten about my walk. Soon I noticed I had attracted a large audience, who were asking me all sorts of questions about what I was doing placing my hand on the small head of that bird. They were quite amazed by the fact that I was able to save that bird from the busy traffic and stop its suffering. I had felt compelled by an inexplicable drive to do what I did. I just could not leave it alone.

The other incident occurred when a bird had flown into a glass window and landed on the balcony of my home when I was living in Africa. As I was watching, I saw how the bird was shaking and struggling with pain, not able to fly again. I went over to the bird and put my hand over its head as is customary when practicing Reiki. I closed my eyes and said, "Please heal this bird from this pain and let it fly again." I genuinely felt bad for the bird and sat with it for a while, performing Reiki. Then I went about my day, although my mind was continually focused on the bird, wondering if it was still struggling. After several hours I went back to my balcony and noticed that the bird was no longer there. I was sure it was better and had flown away, which made me extremely happy.

Even when I was young I could never tolerate the suffering of any living being. I grew disturbed and wanted to find a way to help right away. As an adult, I tend to avoid watching unpleasant television shows or movies that portray excessive violence, injustice, or suffering. I have read that watching these types of programs suppresses our immune system and can harm our autonomic nervous system.

After working with Reiki for some time, I began to physically feel the energy that was passing through my body, and I was able to control its flow and channel it toward anything or anyone who needed help. I concentrated mostly on family members and occasionally on few close friends when requested, but I was not interested in making a career of this healing capacity. Still, when someone requested help with healing, I could not say no, so I agreed. On two occasions I gave Reiki healing to women I knew who were in their final stages of cancer, because they requested it. I knew intuitively at that point that the time had come for them, and I did not believe that Reiki could restore them from what was in their karmic destiny. But I also knew it could definitely heal their emotional state by easing their anxiety, fear, and restlessness, keeping them in peace.

Many times, instead of running to the pharmacy to buy over-the-counter drugs to treat simple ailments, I have preferred using Reiki to alleviate pain or discomfort of many kinds. I have practiced healing myself whenever it was necessary, by intense concentration on any part of my body where I experienced pain, ranging from simple headaches to discomfort or imbalance within the system. I believe that most medications do more harm than good in the long run, and that simple headaches, stomachaches, joint or back pain, even exhaustion can be cured by natural means. Our system in general has the ability to fix itself most of the time. It is a matter of trust and belief; the power of positive thinking always works for me.

My curiosity about healing through energy led me from an interest in Reiki to a deeper sense of wonder about the existence of an inner world. In part, the heat that radiated from my hands, accompanied by the tingling sensation I described earlier, triggered my curiosity. I wanted to know about the very nature of consciousness and how we can direct our innate capacity to reach higher states of consciousness. I started spending a lot of time sitting quietly, practicing concentrating on much higher levels of awareness to find out where all this would lead. By then a kind of inner transformation was beginning to take place that I could not pinpoint, but which manifested as a strong desire to be in quietude. I started meditating actively each day, without any particular method and certainly without a teacher. When friends or coworkers asked me what type of meditation I did, I couldn't answer them. For one thing, I didn't know there were different ways to meditate. I had never become involved in any specific belief system or spiritual practice, although the fact that practicing Reiki had somewhat cleared my inner channels and chakras helped my meditations grow steadily deeper and more effortless.

After I had been meditating for some time, I experienced a certainty that I had never known before—an assurance that my self-transformation was heading in the right direction. I could foresee something about life in general that I really couldn't explain. I sensed a deep knowing that emanated from within, that what was happening was meant to be taken seriously and that I should pursue it. It was something indispensable, without which, I knew, I would not be able to go forward with any sense of completeness.

Over time, during my meditation practices, I learned to move my inner subtle energy with ease. I was able to activate certain chakras and feel the vibration of each of them by concentrating intensely on one particular chakra or area of my body in much the same way as I had learned to heal various pains and ailments in myself. Only after the fact did I learn that the approach to meditation that I'd been following was part of a practice originally known in India as raja yoga. Often called the "royal road" to wisdom, raja yoga comprises a path through meditation that is designed to expand or shift our consciousness to higher levels of union with God. I did not go to any classes or workshops, nor did I speak with others who practiced this form of yoga, but I believe it was chosen for me by the Divine, as it fitted my temperament and mental capacity.

The English word *yoga* comes from a Sanskrit root meaning to unite, or "yoke," and raja yoga links our limited mortal consciousness to Universal, or Cosmic, Consciousness, the ultimate goal of life. Unlike what some believe, though, yoga is not simply a set of physical exercises, bodily movements, and stretches to make us more flexible, help us lose weight, or reduce stress. The form of yoga known as hatha yoga does employ a series of *asanas*, or postures, to keep the mind and body healthy. But raja yoga is based on controlling the mind, because our perception of Self is obscured by disturbances that arise in the mind. If we can still the mind, then the pure Self will be allowed to shine forth. We are all immortal souls using our bodies and minds as instruments to gain experience in this world. Yoga—the ancient art of harnessing the breath and body in service of God—teaches us that the soul must climb back up the ladder of consciousness to Spirit in order to regain the realization of its oneness with the Divine. Our innate Divinity still needs to merge back to its highest form of pure energy or consciousness. Practicing the yoga of meditation helps lift us from ignorance and lead us to Truth.

Raja yoga includes practical techniques that reinforce our intellectual understanding with an *experiential knowing* that leads us to realize the Self beyond the ego and to find the *atman*—the soul. As an integral approach, raja yoga does not simply advocate meditation, but also takes into consideration one's entire life with a practical and scientifically worked out method of reaching the Truth by bringing us to a state of evolutionary preparedness. Systematized some two thousand years ago by the great sage Patanjali, it follows his eight-step method of reaching the highest state of bliss, or union with God, through concentration and meditation.

The first of these eight steps, or "limbs" as he called them, is *yama*, or moral conduct. This consists of maintaining basic moral and ethical qualities, such as abstaining from falsehood, theft, and greed. It emphasizes practicing nonviolence, truthfulness, and compassion for all sentient creatures as well as maintaining integrity and sexual continence.

The second limb is *niyama*, a set of disciplines involving inner and outer purity, contentment, devotion, and religious observances that include the reading and study of sacred scriptures. Together, yama and niyama make up the prerequisites for moving on to higher forms of consciousness. Without them, no practice of yoga will succeed. Niyama, for instance, includes hygienic and dietary rules to prepare our body and mind for the progressive refinement of consciousness needed for meditation, such as cultivating contentment and equanimity of mind.

The third step is known as *asana*, choosing the right postures to still bodily restlessness and gain steadiness. This requires practicing a daily series of exercises to improve posture, because the spine needs to be straight to allow the energy to climb easily. It is not necessary to sit in a lotus position; a comfortable chair may suffice, as long as you develop a posture that is, in Patanjali's words, "firm but relaxed." Failure to do so can create problems in your meditation, because your focus will be on feeling uncomfortable rather than quieting the mind.

Pranayama, the fourth limb, teaches us to control prana, the subtle life current whose most obvious manifestation is the breath that sets the whole system into motion.

The practice of controlled breathing balances the *ida* and *pingala nadis*, two subsidiary energy channels that surround the sushumna, or central channel, together making up the most important invisible nerve system in our subtle body. Breath control is an essential technique on the path to intensive meditation and ultimately to self-realization; I'll go into this practice in more detail in a future chapter.

The fifth limb or stage is *pratyahara*, or "sense control," which involves the withdrawal of the senses from external objects so that they may center on the inner plane. It is like stopping all the traffic of the senses, so that sight, touch, hearing, smell, and taste are pacified or controlled.

Dharana, or concentration, is the technique we use to still the mind's turbulence by fixing its attention on something. You choose an object or location, such as a candle flame or the spot between the eyebrows, on which to focus your unwavering attention as a prelude to entering deeper states of meditation. If the mind wanders from its limited field of attention, it should be brought back gently.

The seventh technique is called *dhyana*, or meditation that we achieve by becoming so absorbed in the object on which we place our attention that we practically become one with it as we realize inwardly the imperturbability of the mind. With a good deal of practice, you learn to keep your attention steady without any distractions or interruptions.

The final stage is *samadhi*, or total absorption in the object of concentration, which leads to a change in quality from gross to subtle. This represents a new mode of consciousness, which I have been calling Self-realization. When the object of our concentration is the Divine, then samadhi amounts to union with God, a merging with Supreme or Universal Consciousness. The meditator, the object of meditation, and meditation itself all merge and our consciousness is fully integrated. There are several levels or kinds of samadhi, which I will describe more fully later in the book. Although it took several years, practicing this method helped me observe and perceive various internal states as I advanced.

Because of persistent concerns about my husband's health, my husband and I decided to stay in the United States and cut back on travel to other countries for business. I returned to the pharmaceutical company where I had worked before and contented myself with my daily routines and my growing practice of meditation. As I spent more time in meditation, I noticed a change in my way of thinking and my outlook on life in general. At the same time, though, a kind of sadness crept up within me that was different from the sorrow I had previously felt for others who were suffering from pain or physical ailments. This time there was no specific reason for the melancholy feeling, so I continued to ignore it and kept busy with my everyday duties. And since I didn't understand this feeling of sadness, I did not mention it to anyone else. Although I spent more and more time meditating, I did not know whether I was really meditating or just sitting quietly and looking for answers. By this time, I had begun to meditate twice a day and had experienced some improvement in stilling my mind. It used to take at least twenty to thirty minutes for all mental activity to subside, but as I increased my practice I was able to reduce the time I needed to become calm. I tried to meditate early in the morning after waking up and then again before I went to sleep. But this was difficult in the midst of a full-time job and my roles as wife and mother. I took care to finish all my tasks prior to meditating, so that I would not be distracted by concerns about what still needed to be done. Initially I stayed up until one or two a.m. so that I could meditate after completing my responsibilities, even on days when I was tired and would have rather gone to sleep. I always meditated with a fixed central aim in mind. I did not want to skip even a single day of my meditation, and this drive to accomplish whatever I set out to do helped me overcome my fatigue.

After I had been meditating for a year and half, becoming ever more deeply immersed in my practice, I began to lose interest in my job. I found it hard to focus on my work when I was more concerned about finding the cause of the sadness within me, not to mention my increasing dissatisfaction with everyday matters. I believed that the thirst for something more would lead me to another level of being, but what that level was or how I would get there, I couldn't even begin to imagine.

Personal Approach to Meditation

Perhaps this is a good place to describe the techniques I follow when I meditate. For me, meditation has never been about sitting in a lotus position with legs crossed and struggling to focus in order to stop thoughts and calm the mind. As I've noted, when I started meditating I didn't take any special classes or follow any particular system, other than the basic principles that most meditators practice. These include keeping the spine straight, with the shoulders slightly back, eyes gently closed, and the awareness focused between the eyebrows. Beyond that, I selected my own methods that were comfortable, as far as sitting was concerned. Because I found the so-called lotus position extremely uncomfortable, I used a simple bamboo stool to sit, keeping my spine straight and legs close together, allowing easy circulation, and hands joined gently in my lap.

Today I no longer use any of the familiar mudras that many people believe help facilitate their meditation. Mudras are symbolic or ritual gestures that originated mainly in ancient India and are still in use throughout the world—for example, making a circle with the thumb and index finger, with the other fingers extended straight out. I have used mudras at times in the past, but gave up the practice because I felt it was not necessary.

What *is* essential is to perform meditation in a clean, secluded place at the same time every day if possible. You should clean your body completely prior to meditation, by taking a shower, putting on clean, comfortable clothing, and having a clean, empty stomach. It's best not to eat before meditation, unless you wait at least three or four hours afterward, so that the digestive system is at least three-quarters empty. Even if you have a busy schedule, it helps to set apart a specific time each day for meditation. Begin with five minutes of meditation, and see if you can add two or three minutes every so often.

After this it's a matter of calming the mind by doing deep breathing for five minutes prior to meditation. (I will describe the particular form of breathing generally known as pranayama in a later chapter.) Then you may choose your own object of concentration or a focal point that is most comfortable for you. It may be your favorite image, the point where your heart is located, or between your eyebrows, but stay with it every time you meditate. I'll have more to say about meditation later in this book.

THREE
Renunciation and Detachment

To the Western mind, the common perception is that renunciation means learning to do without material attachments—a kind of withdrawal from the world to an ashram or monastery, or even to a forest or mountain cave or other desolate place, to pray and to meditate. There is more to it than that! With a husband, two children, and all the responsibilities of a typical householder, while working full-time in the pharmaceutical industry, I did not have the option of moving to some secluded area. I felt bound to perform all the functions required of me, but I did so mechanically and without any enjoyment, all the while feeling extremely sad. I felt like I was living two different lives. What enjoyment or interest I felt came only from spiritual activities and devotion.

This state of anomie eventually became worse. I came to feel like a *sannyasin,* someone who has withdrawn from worldly pleasures and turned mostly toward the Divine, becoming detached from everything and everyone and experiencing a strange disinclination toward all mental or physical entities. The only difference was that I could not leave to take up residence in an ashram or go away to an isolated venue of some kind or stay with any particular guru for an extended time. I never abandoned my family or ignored any of my responsibilities, even though I felt like doing so at times. I lost all interest in spending time with people, shopping, eating, entertainment, or anything that most people look forward to. As my condition progressed, I began to have difficulty even with the continuation of ordinary day-to-day activities. Emotionally I felt drained at times and withdrew from the world as my desire to totally renounce everything and everyone increased. I was constantly dealing with a peculiar inner unrest and a thirst for something more in spite of having everything.

My accustomed wants, desires, and needs were minimized, and my physical appetites withered away. I felt as though I were drowning in a deep well. I was certain that something had altered in my mind, although not in the physical realm. It is a strange feeling not to want or look forward to anything. I have read that this type of "desirelessness" is a preparation for a higher state of consciousness, and when the desires are gone, automatic renunciation happens naturally, inevitably, as in my case. At the time, however, I didn't really understand any of this or what that state was! At times I hated feeling this way and wondered what the reason for all this change could be. I wished that I could return to the way I used to be—not realizing that what was happening was already sacred. Although I seemed normal in every other way to the people around me, I knew I no longer was the same individual that I had been before.

This strange state of feeling went on for almost a year and a half. At times I wondered whether I was depressed or maybe needed to consult a doctor; yet I knew it was not depression, but rather a fascination or strange type of passion for divinity. Because I had never been involved with any spiritual or ritualistic activities, I found this odd indeed. But it felt like something that was preordained and was being imposed on me. I could not talk about this to anyone, especially my family or friends. I felt none of them would understand or be of any help with these concerns. As I struggled with these feelings by myself, eventually I started putting off some of my less important tasks.

I can't explain how odd it felt to know that a radical shift was taking place in my mind regarding the way I viewed life. There seemed to be a dramatic change in my interests, my habits, even my food intake. My energy was withdrawn from everything that required attention to detail, and I preferred being by myself. In my daily life I was no longer turning outward but more and more inward. At the same time, I began forgetting so many things that had happened in the past, including events from my childhood days. It was as though I could remember things from only the most recent past or that had happened just a few days ago. When someone asked me a question, I couldn't hear what they were saying, and I would end up asking "What?" too many times. If my children asked me about something that had happened recently, I would say that I didn't remember; they would get frustrated and make negative comments that I had to ignore.

At first I thought that perhaps something was wrong with my brain; it seemed to undergo a shift from linear to nonlinear thinking. It felt as if it had been rewired and even that my genes had changed their expression. Although I was frustrated at not being able to explain openly what I was going through, I realized that my seeming disorientation must have been caused by my daily deep meditations. I knew there was a definite connection between the physiologic responses in my body and whatever was happening spiritually within me, but I was also disturbed at the level of anxiety and deep restlessness I now felt as I was meditating. I was constantly in a confused state of mind.

Our brain, which has been culturally conditioned for so long, seems to be altered through meditation. As David Hawkins says in his book *Transcending the Levels of Consciousness*, as one moves to a new level of consciousness, "there is a disparity of styles in processing information from linear presentation to nonlinear awareness and when consciousness expands [advanced states of consciousness] so much, all the previous things no longer function well. When mind is silent it no longer processes data in a sequential linear style."

For some time I had experienced my heart racing during and after meditation. I also got alarmingly high blood-pressure readings, along with a sudden gush of heat or concentrated energy and constant vibration and pressure in the area of my forehead referred to as the third eye, which I had never felt before. I also experienced occasional high-pitched ringing in my ears and began smelling rare but delightful fragrances that would come and go during my meditations. Many doctors and psychologists now recommend meditation to control stress and *lower* blood pressure. Yet, ironically, when the inner energy begins to be activated, your blood pressure can spike temporarily, something I didn't know at the time.

With all these apparently inexplicable changes to my consciousness, accompanied by unexpected sensory experiences, the one way I could find peace was by sitting outdoors. Nature became my best friend as well as a kind of entertainment that stimulated my whole system. I had always loved to indulge my mind with sensory impressions created by nature and its beauty, but now I discovered an even greater relaxation and peace simply by sitting and observing the natural scenery.

I was delighted to find that I was able to see the natural colors and auras of every living creation with a new clarity. It became one of my favorite hobbies to spend most of my free time observing nature, especially the various birds of many colors. I even felt as if I were talking with nature, as though I were part of it. At times I talked out loud, saying, "You are no different from me. You took the form of a tree or a bird just as I took this human form, and we both are stuck."

We are all part of this creation of innumerable forms; nature and humanity go hand in hand. When we say we need to abide by the cosmic or universal law, what does that really mean? I think that because nature and we partake of the same universal energy or consciousness, there has to be harmony between the two. Our wrong actions can disturb the operation of cosmic law, which can lead to an imbalance in nature. When everything is in harmony, nature gives immense pleasure to our inner self. Whenever we do not consider ourselves to be part of that, the result is always chaos, dissatisfaction, and restlessness. When we take nature to be part of us and are in tune with its needs, then nature cooperates with us and enhances our spiritual growth. I can't express profoundly enough in words the attachment I have with nature. There is a definite closeness and comfort that I cherish immensely when I am outdoors. I tend to spend every minute of my free time either around the ocean, in various types of gardens, or just in the midst of lush of greenery. It has a tremendous effect on my entire system and uplifts me constantly.

As I have mentioned, I not only like to spend my free time outdoors, but have also come to do my meditations outdoors whenever possible, especially if the sun is shining. Indeed, I'm fairly obsessed with the sun. I find that being in the sun every morning rejuvenates and energizes my entire system. The abundance of cosmic energy it emits is known to cure a wide range of mental or physical problems and is essential for overall well-being. I practically chase the sun by moving to different parts of the world as the seasons change, especially in winter months, so I can be in a sunny climate and always be part of nature. Meditating in front of the sun takes me to higher realms in a matter of minutes.

I can still recall the time when my eye turned red for some unknown reason. I had heard that when certain subtle chakras near the optic nerve are being activated this can happen. However, I was not sure, at the time, what was happening. Apart from having an extremely red eye, I had a great deal of pain and pressure for several days. Because I sensed that my condition was caused by my spiritual practices, including prolonged, intensive meditation, I didn't consider seeing a doctor or using any medication available over the counter. Instead, I decided to go out and sit for an hour in front of the direct sun and meditate. Before I knew it, the pain and pressure had subsided and the redness disappeared. It is amazing what faith can do. I thanked the cosmic power of nature, showing my sincere gratitude for returning my eye to its normal state.

Suddenly one morning, I decided to resign my job, and later the same day I handed in my letter of resignation. Since my husband was still working, there was no financial pressure on me. The question of money never crossed my mind even once; my decision was never based on that. And frankly, at this point I would not have worried even if I hadn't had any money, as my needs had always been modest. My mind was made up that what mattered more to me than anything else was to continue the unfolding of my spiritual path. Even though I enjoyed working and being with people and was proud to have been a part of a worthwhile organization for so many years, I felt it was time to leave. Once I handed in my resignation, I felt that I'd made the best decision possible; I did not experience any regret or disappointment, either then or later. In truth, I felt the job was a hindrance to what I was really after. I felt toward my work pretty much as I did toward the everyday tasks that made up my life at home.

My feeling of detachment was even stronger in regard to the world of technology, with all its high-tech gadgets and multiple operational options. I was never the kind of person who loves constantly upgrading to the latest model cell phone or computer software. Indeed, I became irritated and impatient if something took too much time to figure out or did not function well while I was using it. Strangely, I didn't have any difficulty concentrating on other things, but it seemed as if my left-brain capacity for logical, linear thought had deteriorated. Combined with my declining zest for work, this was enough to make me want to quit my job. My sudden departure came as a total surprise to some of my coworkers and managers, since I hadn't come close to retirement age and had had no trouble with anyone at work. I was so absorbed in my work that I always delivered all that was given to me on time. Even long after resigning, I received occasional calls from my bosses asking me if I would like to come back to work on a part-time basis or as a consultant. Though it felt good to have such an option, I was dead set against going back. It was such a strong decision that there was no wavering or doubt on my part. I knew deep down in which direction I was being driven.

Likewise, my husband, family, and friends had no clue as to what was happening. Most of the time I would act as if nothing was wrong. Since I knew no one could understand, there was no point in explaining. But I couldn't pretend to myself, and I grew increasingly confused. I started actively researching, browsing different texts for accounts of something similar to the state I was experiencing and hoping to locate a spiritual individual I could reach out to. I read the teachings of prominent sages and yogis of ancient times, and of enlightened individuals in recent years who had lifted themselves to higher states of consciousness.

The first book that made a profound impression on me was Patanjali's *Yoga Sutras*, translated by Swami Satchidananda. As mentioned in the previous chapter, Patanjali collated the wisdom of yogis from thousands of years past and presented it with great clarity and simplicity, from the most elementary to the most highly advanced points on the spiritual path. Contrary to common belief, Patanjali wrote not about the specifics of what is known as hatha yoga, the postures and practices so popular in the West today, but simply about the principles required for all spiritual development, of which asana, or posture, is just one small slice.

Whatever internal urge was moving me to read also directed me to a specific *type* of book, as though it was meant for me to read, especially those regarding renowned sages and highly realized mystics. Self-realization has been a subject of fascination among Westerners, at least since the beginning of the twentieth century, when books on the subject first appeared in English. Yet most of those books, and the hundreds written since, simply describe the state itself or the teachings of the many mystics who have experienced it. The books I was driven to read were by or about Sri Ramakrishna Paramahansa, Sri Ramana Maharshi, Swami Muktananda, Sri Nisargadatta Maharaj, J. Krishnamurti, Ramesh Balsekar, Sri Aurobindo and Mother, Sri Chinmayananda, the Dalai Lama, Ken Wilber, David Hawkins, Osho Rajneesh, Gopi Krishna, Paramahansa Yogananda, and many more. Some of these books seemed as though they were specifically picked for me, as if I was to receive certain answers from them. Every one of those embodied souls stimulated me, and some of their concepts and thoughts guided me in such a way as to cause a change in my thinking. Also most of these great souls' teachings brought me profound understanding and inspired me on my own spiritual journey.

As we know, wisdom and knowledge come through many sources: they come from feelings or intuition, through human interaction based on pure reason and logic, and through scientific methods or observations. I feel we gain better understanding by reading and hearing various teachings; they also help us readjust our values, and give us a proper sense of proportion.

I was especially helped by those books written by Swami Muktananda, Gopi Krishna, and the Mother, a woman who was born in France to Turkish and Egyptian parents and became a lifelong disciple of Sri Aurobindo of India. Each of these teachers described in detail various stages of the evolution of consciousness as if they were talking about issues I had been going through myself. I needed confirmation of certain things I'd been struggling with, and reading the right book at the right time gave me great comfort and satisfaction by shedding light on the internal changes that had been occurring within me.

As I read these books, I was astonished at how easy it suddenly seemed to comprehend even the most advanced, complicated philosophical aspects of Divine Truth. I had never been a voracious reader of books other than what was required in college, and so I was surprised to discover that I had read more than a hundred spiritual books in a short period of time—not skimming them but reading every sentence, with total recall. I came to believe that because of my constant meditation, my brain cells had been activated to a point such that I was able to comprehend and absorb much more information than ever before, and with ease. This became another sign for me that some kind of inner evolutionary shift had been taking place, steering me toward a different level of consciousness. It felt as though some deeper aspect of the subtle energy center had suddenly been activated. Although I had been devoting more time to meditation, it also occurred to me that, after many incarnations of this human life, we finally tap into something that allows us to use our highest potential to experience extraordinary capabilities or skills that we have never used before.

The Law of Karma

Over time I understood that we all will be led to the work we are supposed to do in this life, as our evolutionary process unfolds as a result of our previous actions. This is what is known as the law of karma: simply put, our choices and actions and their consequences depend on how we exercise our free will, the God-given resource we all have. The word karma crops up in so many different contexts, from traditional Hindu belief to popular usage in the West, that I need to explain my own understanding of how karma works. We have all probably wondered why bad things sometimes happen to people who are basically good, including ourselves. Why do some people appear to have an easy time of it in this life, being born into abundance with many gifts and talents, while others are born into dysfunctional families or impoverished, violent, disease-ridden societies? It's natural to wonder if some of this apparent imbalance might be the result of karma.

The most basic definition of karma is the law of cause and effect: if we do good, then good will flow back to us; if we do evil, we will eventually suffer the results of our bad actions. This is based on the recognition that humans have the God-given capacity to distinguish between right and wrong in most cases. To the extent that we have free will, we should be able to do the right thing; but since we don't always do so, we pay the karmic consequences.

By this reckoning, if you believe in reincarnation, then you accept that our destiny in this life can be influenced by our good or bad actions in one or more previous lifetimes. But if you believe in free will, then you accept that we have the power to change our destiny by repaying evil with good, dishonesty with truth, and so on. In the Eastern view of karma, each of us carries a bank of memories or impressions (in Sanskrit, *samskaras*) from our past lives into our current life and subsequent lives. These impressions of past acts create our innate tendencies or inclinations (called *vasanas* in Sanskrit), which dictate what we will experience in this life. The differences in the texture of our inner tendencies are part of what makes us unique individuals. Those tendencies may also evoke a sense of familiarity in certain situations that we encounter, which in turn may predispose us to act in a certain manner. When that happens, we are responsible for deciding to follow our tendencies to do good and to resist tendencies to act in an evil or selfish manner.

By choosing not to repeat prior bad actions and to act instead in a more generous, compassionate way, we can alter the course of our karma. For instance, if you know you have a tendency toward anger that often leads you to say or do harmful things to others, you have two choices. If you remain willfully ignorant and keep giving in to your angry outbursts, each expression of anger will strengthen your tendency to have another outburst. In time you may alienate friends and loved ones or even commit an act of violence that leads to dire consequences. Or you may choose to heighten your awareness of your tendency toward anger and find ways to ameliorate it, for instance, by undergoing some form of anger-management counseling.

Another way to develop your ability to consistently choose right over wrong is through effort, by elevating your consciousness to a higher order. Swami Abhedananda, a direct disciple of the Bengali saint Sri Ramakrishna, once wrote, "Just as every effect must have a cause, every consequence must have an antecedent, so also there must be equal balance between a cause and its effect, between an antecedent and a consequence. A cause must always produce an effect of similar nature both in quality and quantity and reaction must be similar to the action."[2]

Since the power of the Divine and our individual free will are bound together, our ability to make the right choice depends to some extent on divine guidance. Our given life is nothing more than a cosmic drama that has already been written. It's true that we have free will, but it serves us only as long as we abide by the cosmic law and remain in tune with Divine Truth. Otherwise, free will can lead us to get frustrated, because we need constant divine intervention. The Divine is the prime mover and absolute decision maker, and under its control each of us enjoys free will in our limited sphere. Our free will is enhanced when we recognize divine guidance within ourselves.

God intervenes, deciding retribution according to what best suits the spiritual growth of each of us. Ultimately the Divine dispenses the fruits or selects the consequences of activities that we must undergo in each lifetime, according to our merits and demerits. However, I believe that the Divine also considers the conscious effort we put toward making the right choice. Evolution demands change, and making different decisions by using our free will alters our life so that we can attain better outcomes and evolve consciously.

"Fate and free will co-exist and actually work together to facilitate ongoing evolutionary growth," says evolutionary astrologer Donna Lee

Steele.[3] According to the natural law of karma, every choice made or action taken has a corresponding outcome. Our ability to make the right choice depends on our current evolutionary stage. When we choose values that are conducive only to our self-interest without responsibility for others, we generally end up with a negative result. Also, since we deal with reason and senses, the ability to exercise our *free will* correctly decreases; this diminshment may lead to actions contrary to the cosmic law and produce a wrong outcome.

As the saying goes, "As you sow, so shall you reap."

So we are presented with a kind of catch-22. We have to evolve to a higher level in order to make the right choices and grow in consciousness. But if we don't evolve, we keep making the same *wrong* decisions, which create more negative karma. This tends to reinforce our tendency to keep making selfish decisions, leading to still more negative karmic consequences. It's a little like the alcoholic who keeps going to the same bar and getting drunk instead of going to a meeting or getting counseling. We can handle our negative karmic tendencies only when we exercise our free will consciously and correctly, with vigor and persistence, to an extent that is needed to bear fruit.

So, in the end we are the builders of our own destiny for better or for worse; we are the architects of our own life, of the human evolutionary process that is taking place within all of us. We evolve back to perfection by exercising our *free will* appropriately. The best solution to the dilemma of karma is to raise ourselves to a higher state of consciousness and attain realization of our True Self. Once we are Self-realized, all our karma is removed.

The use of our free will to improve our karma may sound like pulling ourselves up by our own bootstraps. In a sense it is, but we can also use all the help we can get. I continued to search for someone with whom I could speak regarding these kinds of conundrums. Even though I was satisfied with my reading and my practice of meditation, I still wanted to find an illumined teacher to talk to. At times I felt that some kind of awakening had occurred within me, although I did not really understand the meaning of awakening. As I researched the subject, I found certain parallels to my situation, including references to a marked increase in one's intuitive sense. I also knew that my inner energy had been awakened and that I needed to learn how to manage this development. I was growing frustrated, desperate to have a sincere dialogue with someone who knew more than I did.

At the same time, I knew that I was supposed to do something more. I didn't believe that I had to change my existing situation, which included being a wife and mother, with all the day-to-day responsibilities of a typical householder. Changing places or abandoning your circumstances is not a solution, though some believe it is. Finally I came to the conclusion that only a highly realized individual would understand what was happening within me. I started looking into this diligently, with the intention of finding a teacher with whom I could have a dialogue in person.

Finding a Teacher

There is an old saying, "When the student is ready, the teacher will appear." Gurus are necessary at some point in the journey of those who are striving to achieve awareness of their True Self. But with so many teachers from a wide range of traditions, it can seem hard to know who is the right teacher for you. The simplest way to know would be to sit a few minutes with a teacher and sense whether you can feel peace of mind in his or her presence, along with a natural sense of respect. You should also pay attention to whether their teachings resonate with the beliefs, traditions, and practices that most powerfully align with your personal spiritual style. As you continue to follow a particular teacher, be alert to whether you are being asked to do anything that feels wrong, manipulative, or disrespectful. We'll see more about this in the following chapter.

FOUR
Meeting My Guru

Even as I was practicing my daily meditation, I was not aware of the many spiritual teachers that existed, and so I didn't dream of visiting one at that time. I later observed that many people consult such teachers, or gurus, to help resolve conflicts regarding personal relationships, career, and all the confusions of daily life that they appear to be incapable of handling themselves. Yet I don't believe that gurus are here for that purpose. Nor do I believe that they can lead us to Self-realization if we are not already seeking it. No teacher, no scripture, no book can do that for us. Only we can attain the self-knowledge that comes with deep meditation. It is like going to a school and applying what we learn. We don't learn just by sitting in class and listening to the teacher; we have to go home and study, putting in time and hard work. The effort is what gets us to our goal.

Further, a guru's destination can't be our destination. Their agenda can't be our agenda. Although gurus do have practical wisdom to offer, their primary function is to show us the correct spiritual path and provide the knowledge and tools we need when we are ready to proceed on the journey to realization, inspiring us to proceed with confidence. They have a definite purpose and a goal of their own to fulfill, as we all do. It could be elevating other souls that are ready, or perhaps assisting those who are struggling to bring improvement to impoverished societies. A highly illumined teacher serves not only to instruct, but also to activate the inner energy of the devotee, which facilitates the spiritual journey of the disciple from limited awareness to unlimited awareness of Truth, which has been obscured by illusion.

I had read that when a devotee truly is ready to take the path to attain divine realization, the Divine sends a spiritual teacher to show the way. I believed this happens automatically because this special teacher is like a messenger of our real Self. A highly illumined teacher who is established in Supreme Consciousness and has seen the Divine directly is the primary source of spiritual information on our path. Finding the right guru is similar to working with a good sports coach, a sponsor or therapist for alcoholism or drug addiction, or a highly educated professor to help us obtain an advanced degree. Along with imparting knowledge, a guru also removes obstacles on the path and inspires us to put forth maximum effort. Without a spiritual teacher, we are unlikely to make sufficient progress toward reaching higher states of consciousness. According to the great yogi Paramahansa Yogananda, "A true God-illumined guru is one who, in his attainment of self-mastery, has realized his identity with the omnipresent Spirit. Such a one is uniquely qualified to lead the seeker on his or her inward journey toward divine realization."[1]

It is as if we are climbing a ladder and the teacher makes sure that the ladder is free of any barriers that might impede our progress. When the devotee is ready, for instance, only a fully enlightened master can activate the inner energy known as kundalini. Another of their functions is to explain the divine essence of Truth, out of which realization will come to those who are prepared to receive it.

We have to be careful to identify the right spiritual teacher, because some who present themselves as gurus are merely seeking to exploit the gullible. The saying I alluded to earlier, about the teacher appearing when the student is ready, begs the question of how we can know for sure not only who is a genuine teacher, but also which one is right for us. Once I realized that I would need a personal teacher, I came to believe in my heart that the right teachers are the ones who call upon those souls who are ready to attain realization.

Amma with Sarada in conversation at the ashram in India.

The most powerful teachers project such a high-energy field that their state of consciousness is uplifting in itself. This is why, when you meet the teacher who is meant for you, you will feel the vibrations. It is as if the teacher's energy field aligns with yours. This was true in my case; for many years I made no conscious effort to find a teacher, and yet when the appropriate one appeared, I was strongly drawn toward her much as I had been drawn to each step along my path.

Some seekers believe that gurus live in a special world, out of touch with everyday reality, but this only reveals our lack of knowledge of the spiritual world. In the past, following the journey to higher states of consciousness meant either joining a religious order, retreating to a monastery or ashram, or wandering in the forests abandoning the responsibilities of the given life. Though certain mystics may have led the secluded, self-absorbed life of a hermit, I am sure this was a personal decision and is not the criterion of a true master. Today's model of enlightenment is being reshaped to offer new ways of incorporating intensive spiritual growth while leading one's given life.

Likewise, there seems to be a misconception that spiritual awakening—achieving realization or enlightenment—is a rare occurrence that happens to only a chosen few who have been on the spiritual path for many years. But I do not believe that, nor do I agree with those who think they need to go away to some secluded place for a period of time, renouncing everything of the material world. Instead of saying *chosen*, I prefer to say that students are *ready*, because the experience of oneness is within the reach of anyone who is ready for it. Because the purpose of human existence is to awaken and eventually attain realization of the Self within, the universe has ordained that all of us will reach the goal sooner or later.

The Indian Connection

Although I have been living in the West since the age of fourteen, my cultural roots and way of thinking about spirituality reflect the Eastern traditions into which I was born. When I began my search for spiritual realization, I was still very much influenced by the Indian culture in

Sarada visiting with Amma at the ashram.

which I had spent the first years of my life, in which the primacy of the spiritual in everyday life is much older and more deeply rooted than in Western countries. India has never lost contact its ancient spiritual and yogic roots or its civilization, which dates back many thousands of years. India and other ancient cultures have always given great importance to attaining higher consciousness and authentic spiritual knowledge, as evidenced by their customs and way of life. The central theme of India's spiritual message to the world has always been the importance of the unfoldment of the higher Self. As Yogananda writes in *Journey to Self-Realization*:

> The real life and secret of India's vitality is her spiritual culture, from time immemorial, which has made her the motherland of religions. . . As the spiritual model of all religions, India has been the un-proclaimed reformer, the grand inspirer of human minds and souls. Her greatest and richest legacy to mankind has been the techniques for the scientific spiritual culture of man, discovered and handed down through the centuries by her saints and seers.[2]

The great yogis and mystics have, after all, always sought to realize Supreme Consciousness through meditation practices. However, I've also learned that Easterners tend to be reticent to describe their experience of the transformational changes that seekers can expect to face on the path. I have always wondered why so many in India hold certain aspects of realization to be sacred and secret, and why this inner knowledge has by and large been kept between disciple and teacher over the centuries. I feel there is no need for such secrecy, because first-hand accounts of what to expect are of utmost value to those on the spiritual journey. And in recent years, a number of Indian masters have come forward to share their wisdom and experience with the rest of the world, from Yogananda himself to the likes of Maharishi Mahesh Yogi, Ramana Maharshi, Swami Satchitananda, and many more.

Without question India has the longest history, among all the cultures we know about, of exploring the spiritual dimension. "India's real place in the world," writes American Hindu author David Frawley, "is not in becoming another materialistic nation like those of the West but in showing the way to a civilization based on spiritual freedom and oneness with both nature and God."[3]

Once I became aware of the role of spiritual teachers, I wanted an illumined being who had attained the highest wisdom and knowledge, and I specifically preferred a teacher who came from the Indian tradition. I was also looking for someone who, like the ancient sages and mystics, not only had achieved the highest level of illumination, but also could express that knowledge in ways that could be easily understood by anyone who was ready. So when I learned that an enlightened sage from Southern India was coming to the United States, where she had become known for satisfying the spiritual and emotional needs of her Western followers, I began to read and inquire about her. I further discovered that she was exactly what I was looking for, an authentic Indian sage who advocated following all the scriptures of India and who guided her followers to reach higher states of consciousness through meditation, yoga, and breath control. After learning this I made up my mind to go see her.

Amma Karunamayi, popularly known as Amma, offers instruction and guidance in meditation, which attracted me because I had already been on that path for some time. Her teachings focus mostly on Cosmic Consciousness, which manifests as the Divine Mother of all creation, sometimes called Divine Shakti. Since I was already reading extensively in Eastern spirituality, I understood a great deal of what she teaches. She emphasizes the necessity of purifying the chakras using tools including pranayama and yoga, along with the sun's solar energy and proper diet, to reach the ultimate union with Universal Oneness. I learned further that her teachings focused on developing the inner virtues of compassion, truthfulness, devotion, contentment, and unconditional love to produce a state of mind conducive to deep meditation. "To know the Self," she says, "is the sole purpose of our life."

The seven main chakras, which lie along the central energy channel, are situated not in the gross body, but in the subtle, or etheric, body—a kind of energy sheath that surrounds and interpenetrates the physical body. Although these chakras are designed to function naturally with divine energy from birth, they are covered over by our karmic deeds of this and innumerable previous lifetimes, as if obscured by a thick layer of dust that needs to be purified. This karmic blockage prevents the inner dormant energy—the kundalini that is in the base of the spine—from ascending and leading us to realize our full potential or our inner sense of life purpose. I had read that this woman was teaching how one could progress to a higher consciousness by employing the necessary tools to clean up our chakras, among other techniques.

In researching Karunamayi, I learned that she was also giving individual blessings and talking to people one-on-one. This interested me the most, as I had been eager for some time to speak to someone about my questions regarding the spiritual path I had entered. I decided to attend a discourse in the New Jersey area near where I live and to meet her at her individual blessing time, hoping she would clear up my confusion and tell me exactly what was going on with me. Before our first meeting, I was given a card to write down what it was that I wanted to discuss with her. I remember writing the following: "I have been very confused and restless for the past two years and I am hanging in the middle, neither here nor there."

When I finally met Amma, I greeted her with affection and love and gave her the card with my question. She looked right into my eyes with a beautiful smile and spoke with me as though she had known me for a long time. To my surprise she said that she had been expecting me. She already knew why I was there and was aware of what I had been going through for several months. She explained precisely what had been happening as a result of my meditations and answered each of my questions.

I felt very much at ease talking to her in our native language, but before I could ask any more questions I realized that she had already cleared up all the doubts that I had been carrying for so long. She asked me if I could come to her ashram in Southern India to practice deep meditation intensively. Why she wanted me to go there was not entirely clear at that moment, but she did explain that by "deep meditation," she was referring to hours and hours of meditation practice as a task that needed to be completed without interruption, in a sincere manner. She emphasized that I needed to do this now, then pointed out something even more important—that my path toward this stage was bound to happen because it was a continuation of my past-life effort. She clearly stated that I had to finish this and advised me to follow a serious practice of deep meditation, which she called *sadhana,* for an extended period of time.

Once she explained my situation in those terms, it suddenly made a lot of sense. By then I was well versed in the meaning of karma, reincarnation, and the purpose of existence. I knew from that point on that a mystical connection existed between Amma and me, and this intuitive knowing confirmed that I did not need to search for any other teachers. I was determined to do what I was destined to do, regardless of the difficulties I might face in the process. It was no longer just a theory or something I had read about. Instead it was something I would be pursuing personally, as I could distinctly feel some kind of force that was driving me to fulfill this task.

In the beginning I had wondered why I was being drawn toward Amma Karunamayi, as opposed to many other gurus who were teaching publicly. After I had known Amma for a while, I asked her point blank in one of our conversations. Without a moment's hesitation, she told me that she had called me. She explained that spiritual teachers become aware of potential students and begin to send messages to the students to attract them. Being called by a God-realized soul is not something to be taken lightly! I felt as if a big load I had been carrying for a long time had been taken off my shoulders now that I had found the spiritual master I was looking for. I was truly ecstatic. Finally some advice and guidance! With all this in mind, I arranged to go to her ashram for a two-week retreat of intensive meditation.

Retreats and Workshops

It's easy to feel overwhelmed by the variety of spiritual retreats, workshops, and conferences available today. There are no set guidelines for picking and choosing which retreat or workshop one should attend; you should choose a retreat or workshop according to your own understanding of what you want or need.

You may be trying to gain knowledge about higher states of consciousness or how to meditate with an intention of attaining spiritual growth. You may want to learn a specific practice, to socialize with other like-minded souls, or simply to be in the presence of various sages with the hope that you may discover an appropriate teacher. You need to ask yourself what your needs are and at what stage you are in your development. At least make sure you choose a retreat or workshop that gives your life meaning, purpose, and direction.

In the next chapter I'll discuss my own personal experience and address some of these issues in detail.

FIVE
My First Visit to an Ashram

After talking to Sri Amma Karunamayi, I decided almost immediately to go and visit her ashram in India. I knew that she gives a meditation retreat every year and I made sure I attended that year. I finally had something to look forward to, and I started planning for my trip to India just to visit the ashram. I had never heard of this ashram when I was growing up in that part of India, but I learned that this is where a number of India's ancient sages had meditated for many hundreds of years. I was sure the high vibrations exuded by their meditations still remained as they were during the sages' presence, and this knowledge only increased my eagerness to go and meditate there.

I was filled with such uplifting energy, hope, and enthusiasm that I never had any hesitation about being in an ashram for the first time. Until then I had never quite understood what makes people visit these places. But now, deep down, I knew why I was going. I wanted an opportunity to perform many hours of meditation under divine protection and guidance and at the same time be in the presence of a highly illumined holy person. I was sure it would be much more powerful than meditation done alone. I wanted to see and be near Amma again, and with an eager heart I set out for the ashram for my first two-week intensive meditation retreat.

The Penusila Ashram was built in the middle of a forest and between mountains, with nothing but nature surrounding it. Located in the state of Andhra Pradesh in the south of India, it's not an easy place to get to, as you first need to fly to a nearby city and from there endure a five-hour car ride along bumpy, dusty roads, fending off bullock carts, goats, water buffaloes, and flocks of people. Pedestrians go about their business without thinking twice that they are in the middle of hectic traffic; others sell their local food and products from roadside stands. Some areas don't even have actual roads to follow. Amazingly, no one seems to be bothered by any of this.

Once I arrived at the ashram and entered through the gates, I was instantly captivated by the serenity of the place amid all that natural beauty. I felt that I was in a special spiritual atmosphere, a place of silence and an idyllic setting for deep spiritual practice in the presence of an enlightened teacher. Indeed, I realized that this represented a whole new world unlike anything I had ever been exposed to. In short, it was exactly what I was looking for, and being there lifted my energy level. I was certain that being close to Amma and listening to her would give me strength to accomplish my goal. And I realized why she had requested that I come to the Ashram to meditate; the conditions and environment would be utterly conducive to my practice.

The area surrounding her ashram seemed to have a higher concentration of impoverished people than elsewhere. These poor villagers battle such difficulties as drought, lack of health care, and a shortage of primary education. To help alleviate their difficulties, Amma constructed a hospital and several schools and other facilities near the Penusila Ashram.

The building where I was given a room was somewhat like a college dorm, but containing only the bare essentials, and with men and women housed separately. The rooms were about twelve by fifteen feet, with two beds in each room and an attached bath shared by both occupants. The two small beds came with a unique type of mattress made out of a substance resembling jute, an affordable natural fiber second only to cotton in durability. My small pillow appeared to have been used by many over the years. We brought our own necessities such as towels,

Amma's ashram in southern India.

blankets, soap, toiletries, and so on. As the ashram was in the middle of a forest, it could be quite muggy and uncomfortable at times, despite the ceiling fan in each room. During the months of December and January, though, the climate is pleasant and tolerable.

But the relative comfort of the rooms was of little matter anyway, because most of the time I was either meditating or attending the discourses that Amma was giving. My sleeping time was limited, as we needed to be up around four a.m. each day to prepare for the first early meditation session, which started at five. I also had trouble adjusting to showering at that hour, especially since there was no hot water most of the time. Again, though, none of this mattered, as my focus was completely on what I needed to accomplish. All I cared about was taking my meditations to a higher level and listening to what Amma had to say in the two weeks I was going to spend there.

After being there for several days, I had adjusted to the place quite nicely. But then I started noticing things about the other participants' intention for being there that I found disconcerting, to say the least. Perhaps naively, I had thought that everyone was there for the same reason I was—to learn meditation and to elevate their spiritual level. Even though each individual might be at a different spiritual level, I assumed that their goal must be the same. I was soon to learn that the people there had come with diverse intentions, personalities, attitudes, and behavior patterns. Astonishingly, only a few had what appeared to be a genuine intention of attaining spiritual growth. One person who sat next to me in our daily discourse asked me, "How many in this crowd do you think are actually awakened and are here to elevate themselves?" I was trying to grasp exactly what she meant when she answered her own question: "No one."

Later I realized that she was right. At least some of the people, for instance, had come there to resolve various personal issues in their lives. These ranged from trying to get over a bad relationship to coping with physical or emotional health issues, to extreme loneliness or simply wanting an escape from all the personal dirty laundry they did not want to deal with. They saw the ashram as a sanctuary from their personal problems and shortcomings, hoping simply to get some answers and gratification by being close to an enlightened spiritual teacher. I observed that some of the retreat participants also lived there full-time, as they either were given free room and board or had to pay only a small fee.

This isn't to say that these individuals may not have gotten some beneficial instruction and perhaps achieved some insights themselves. Yet to my mind this was not the ultimate purpose for ashrams, which was to create an environment in which people can meditate and learn to uplift their spiritual lives. Worse yet, I sensed that some of the people seemed to be there to satisfy a hunger for personal power that they could not fulfill in the outside world. Still others behaved in an artificial manner, showing diplomatic kindness without any genuine feeling. And for some it was all about boosting their egos. They did this by constantly exhibiting their so-called dedication, by going into an artificial trance-like state or exhibiting peculiar body movements and physical gestures. Perhaps they intended to show that they were more saintly than others.

Because this particular annual retreat is designed for Westerners, they made up most of the ashram's population at this time, apart from Amma's siblings, a handful of local volunteers, and nonresident Indians from the United States and other countries. A few other Westerners had taken on positions of authority at the ashram, running the daily operations and overseeing access to Amma. These people embodied the more aggressive style of the West and of America in particular. They appeared to have taken control on their own, and constantly interfered with the business of other retreat members and devotees, dictating what to do and what not to do in every aspect of ashram life, without any shame. They may have thought that they were impressing Amma, but the fact is that she was involved only in giving her talks and occasionally meeting with retreatants to answer their questions about spiritual practice. Though she was perhaps aware of certain happenings, I felt she did not concern herself with the mundane issues of running the ashram on a daily basis. Two of Amma's sisters and her brother also played roles involving aspects of managing the ashram and overseeing other projects, but not running the retreat schedule itself.

Amma is gone from the ashram much of the year, and as in any bureaucracy, the functionaries tend to take over. I recall one incident when one Western woman would even wear saris of the same color and style as the teacher, to the extent that visitors occasionally mistook this woman for Amma herself! At first I tried to ignore these domineering sorts of people, but I had so many questions for Amma that I couldn't abide their stopping me from approaching her. "No, no, you can't see Amma now," one of her self-appointed guardians told me. "It's not the time to ask questions."

Thanks to my own will power and my personal mentality in general, I always found a way to approach Amma and get my questions answered, by disregarding all the irrelevant happenings around me and moving on toward fulfilling my own agenda. Growing up in the United States for so many years, I myself had acquired a bit of Western tenacity. So one day, as these functionaries were trying to shoo me away, I simply ignored them and approached Amma to address her with all my questions. The fact that Amma and I spoke the same language (Telugu) surely came in handy. She responded in kind and I got all the answers I wanted. After that, I got the access I desired and never really had a problem with those people again. I didn't mention them to Amma initially, not feeling it was my place to do so, but she must have heard from others, and in time the role of those devotees became less prominent.

The two-week meditation retreat started with Amma's introductory discourse and an orientation. Here I became accustomed to the proper meditation regimen, and I felt comfortable following Amma's guidance. She gave a discourse twice a day, which I followed attentively. She discussed the importance of sacred chants, Sanskrit mantras, and various techniques and practices that help aspirants to make meditation more powerful and profound. The day started with morning meditation at five a.m., for sixty to ninety minutes, which was repeated in the afternoon and again in the evening. This schedule was strictly followed in the ashram, but I never abided by a similar schedule when I was away from there. You don't necessarily have to meditate in the early morning, although it is helpful to those that are starting to meditate, as there is more cosmic energy in the atmosphere then. But each of us has our own preference and should choose what suits us the best. In my case, rising early was not necessary, because I was able to attain the proper meditative state at any time of day. Fortunately, I did not face issues such as spiritual lethargy or falling asleep during meditation sessions, perhaps because I had already been meditating for several years. Initially I felt exhausted with the new regimen of long sittings, yet this was the very kind of discipline I wanted and needed, so I went with it.

The good news was that I didn't have to think about or attend to any of my usual household responsibilities. All I had to do was listen, meditate, eat a bit, and rest. Though the amount of time allotted for sleep was limited in contrast to what I was accustomed to at home, still it did not matter. I put all my energy and attention into the meditation sessions and tried to participate in all three sessions with utmost interest and enthusiasm. I was eager to attend Amma's two daily discourses, because everything she said had tremendous impact on me. I not only listened to every word that came out of her mouth, but also put those words into practice immediately. I loved listening to her talk about ancient Indian scriptures and appreciated her practical instructions on incorporating traditional Vedic practices into our daily lives.

Amma also discussed our relationship to nature and the elements, and its effect on reaching higher states of consciousness. She explained how important the sun is for energizing the seven chakras and helping us keep the mind balanced while we meditate. I learned about the influence of sattvic foods on our mind and body and on our meditation process. Sattvic foods are mainly vegetarian, with few of the spices that can overstimulate the system, along with some yogurt and butter or ghee.

Reaching the One-Pointed State

After applying all the tools that Amma provided, I was able in a relatively short time to reach what is called the "one-pointed state." The basic definition of the one-pointed state is one in which the mind places its full, undistracted attention on one object. In this condition, we are able to keep our mind under control without any conscious effort. In my practice, the object of attention was the so-called third eye, also known as the Christ consciousness center, which is located between the eyebrows. In this state of complete absorption, the mind is free of all external and internal distractions. With repeated practice, we are able to apprehend the object we focus on with utmost clarity. In time this kind of prolonged focus or concentration will take us to a clear awareness of Self and result in a total stillness of consciousness, or bliss.

One sign of single-pointedness that I experienced is that the brain feels extremely heavy—as if it is getting rid of all defects of mind and preparing to stabilize the mind to reach emptiness or clear awareness. As a result of this we generate physical and mental bliss. In time the heaviness dissipates and a calm energy circulates throughout the body, creating physical flexibility, removing all bodily concerns, and keeping the body comfortable and stable enough to continue meditation.

Divine Calling

With this two-week intensive, my serious practice of sadhana had begun, and I could feel an inexplicable call, orchestrated by a deep yearning within, pushing me along on this journey. My name for it is the divine calling, while others call it an awakening, a faint glimpse of nondual reality or oneness, or simply a shift in consciousness, an opening of the door toward something much deeper. When this happens one should follow through without ignoring it or putting it off.

I have heard that some people who experience an awakening or a shift in perception don't know what to do about it and so do not move any further. Unless they find ways to have this nondual awareness more frequently, they tend to ignore it and go on with their lives as usual. Unless you are destined to Self-realize, you will not follow through; you have to be receptive to all the signs that the Divine sends.

As you may be wondering what those signs are, I would like to list some that I have personally experienced. These may include any of the following:

- abrupt loss of interest in materialistic things, daily duties, and personal care;
- a sudden loss of appetite or sleep, and increased restlessness;
- intense interest in attending spiritual discourses and visiting sanctuaries and places of worship;
- continuously looking to participate in ritualistic activities;
- a desire to read a wide variety of spiritual books, looking for answers; and wanting to associate with holy and enlightened beings.

As Swami Muktananda once wrote, "The mystical path is best not taken. But once begun, there is no turning back." He understood that unless you are willing to make the commitment, you are better off sticking to your secular life, and that what happens after the awakening will determine the course of your life. An awakening matures into much deeper understanding as you progress further in your journey to reach the goal. I used to wonder what causes this "evolutionary drive" in us. One explanation I have heard is that it is the effect of meditation carried on in previous lifetimes. It may also be activated by inner discipline and a way of life that attunes the brain to that state of higher consciousness. The reason didn't matter to me; I had decided to pursue the path to the end in this life.

Once I resolved to pursue that goal, I knew I had a lot of work ahead of me. I felt strongly that I should not throw away the opportunity that God had given me but follow through until the thirst could be satisfied. It reminded me of what a modern-day Zen teacher, Adyashanti, once said during a retreat I was attending: "Many are called, few respond." I was determined to be one of the responders, and that sense of determination had a soothing effect, imbuing me with a calmness that I had never felt before. It felt as though an enormous power of the Divine was aligned perfectly with my intension and moving me forward to accomplish what was to be done, without any obstacles on the way.

It helped that I liked being in Amma's company. As I mentioned in a previous chapter, when one is ready to take the journey toward Self-realization, a teacher will definitely appear; somehow a guru will find you. While I was in the ashram, I came to realize for the first time that many other teachers were out there, and that people on the path I had chosen usually spend time with several of them. However, until my first visit to the ashram, I was a novice. It was as though all of a sudden a whole new life that I never knew existed opened up for me. I had a preconceived idea that once you *did* find your teacher, it would be disloyal to visit others and partake in their teachings. But after I had taken retreats at Amma's ashram several times, I became aware of other saints, teachers, or realized beings whom many seekers visit frequently, and that it is perfectly all right to do so. I understood that although one guru's teachings may resonate more with you, and you naturally want to stay with that guru, still that need not keep you from visiting and listening to others. It is not unlike the case of aspiring musicians or artists who study with different teachers to expand the range of their knowledge and ability.

Besides Amma Karunamayi, I came to hear about many other teachers who give retreats and workshops, and soon my curiosity led me to partake occasionally in various discourses and conferences while keeping Karunamayi as my main guru. I found it stimulating and inspiring to listen to other teachers, coming to believe that we gain a kind of insight even by discerning who is genuine and who is not. I appreciated the ease and simplicity with which some of these teachers delivered the information based on their experiences. With a few of them, however, I felt that although they might be certain of having found the Truth at the moment of their realization experience, their interpretation of the insights they claimed to have received were not clear, probably because they were conditioned by their own personal philosophy.

But there was one I especially enjoyed listening to: the man I mentioned above, named Adyashanti, an American spiritual teacher from the San Francisco Bay Area. Born Steven Gray, Adyashanti spent time studying with a number of Zen masters and developed his own response to enlightenment. He believes that you can be enlightened and still experience anger, regret, envy, sorrow, grief, depression, even hatred—which is not exactly the standard approach of traditional spiritual teachers. But I found him accessible and was able to understand what he was saying without any difficulty, which was refreshing.

Attending conferences and workshops like Adyashanti's also gave me an opportunity to meet with like-minded people and share conversations that might be somewhat different from those I had with the people I met at Amma's ashram. But I never had any doubt or questions regarding my choice in accepting Amma as my guru and did not see the need to shop around for other teachers. As I've said, I experienced a strong intuitive knowing that she was the right teacher for me and that our meeting had been destined to happen. Indeed, I loved the ambiance of the ashram so much at times that I used to fantasize about how it would be if I just lived there forever and forgot about everything and everyone else.

I have heard that when one is on a spiritual journey or destined to begin one, there can be a tendency to leave home and family and remain in solitude. But I don't feel this is necessary. It may be true that some of the great spiritual masters did leave their families for a time, like the Buddha and Jesus, but even they returned to work with others. Some spiritual individuals may not like living in a conventional setting and may prefer to avoid contact with those who might give them trouble. But although this thought has come to me at times, I have known all along that I could not do that. I have always believed that if one is driven to take this path, one need not abandon one's given life and responsibilities. We can realize Truth only if we continue with our life well-grounded and with all the laundry that comes with it, learning to manage the ups and downs of daily life and relationships. Withdrawing from our active life to enter a monastery or mountain cave may cause complications and disturbance instead of bringing peace. Avoidance of situations, environments, or people does not bring about Self-realization. Eventually the inner knowledge we gain must be integrated with its outer expression while we continue with what Jon Kabat-Zinn, the American doctor and teacher of mindfulness-based stress reduction calls "full catastrophe living."[2]

By the end of second week of the retreat I was feeling adjusted and comfortable with everything. I always had a million questions to ask, mainly regarding how to elevate ourselves to a higher state of consciousness. Along with the times that Amma was teaching, I would seek her out even when we were on breaks so that I could immediately clarify any questions that had arisen. I felt as though I wanted to use every second efficiently, and I so enjoyed speaking with her.

Some people try many different workshops and teachers before they find one that resonates with them. There's nothing wrong that. You can learn a lot about different aspects of the spiritual path from all kinds of workshops and retreats. But as I said regarding the right teacher for you, you will know when you find that person. I'm not recommending one teacher or one set of workshops or retreats over another. Until you get the feel for the right one, it is okay to meet with different spiritual masters and teachers. For instance, I studied Reiki and went to several talks and a silent retreat with Adyashanti. Yet I ended up resonating more intensely with Karunamayi, and I stayed with her. It could be just the opposite for you. It really doesn't matter, because you'll know the one that's right for you.

SIX
Shaktipat, Prana, and Devotion

During the course of the retreat, I discovered that, along with meditation, Amma offered ways to uplift and guide those on the path of realization, depending on their temperament or mental capacity. This is mainly because not all seekers are capable of or interested in pursuing a meditative path. The mind is so restless that it can be overwhelming to confront all the obstacles created by its fluctuation. Because it takes so much patience and perseverance to bring the mind under control, many devotees choose other methods of attaining knowledge.

The ancient spiritual traditions have handed down certain ritualistic practices that have the power to attract divine cosmic energy for the benefit of the practitioner. And so Amma also encourages all sorts of rituals and promotes bhakti yoga, the natural way to divine knowledge through love and devotion for God. This path comprises various forms of idol worship that involve chanting holy scriptures, devotional songs, and sacred mantras, along with other religious practices. According to Amma, each of these ritual practices can evoke spiritual elevation in those who participate. We can attain realization or the awareness of the infinite in many ways. According to Indian philosophy there are four basic forms of yoga in which we can open ourselves to attain divine knowledge:

- jnana yoga, an intellectual approach through self-inquiry, as practiced by Ramana Maharshi, based on the knowledge that remains when we reject everything else as transient and unreal;
- karma yoga, the way to God through selfless actions and service;
- dhyana, or raja yoga, the path of meditation and advanced spiritual practices; and
- bhakti yoga, the path of love and devotion for God.

During the early stages of my own journey, I performed some of the ritualistic practices that are beneficial, although I was not always keen on them. I attended and participated in *homas* (fire ceremonies) and *pujas* (devotional services) performed by Amma and her devotees. Among the most ancient rituals of India, the homa is a sacred fire ceremony in which various forms of divine energy are invoked according to the guidelines in the Vedic scriptures. This tradition involves many Sanskrit mantras that are chanted to the fire god, Agni, who represents the sacred nature of the universe and of our soul as a part of the Divine. The combination of energies of the fire and the mantras creates extremely auspicious and purifying vibrations beneficial to all. According to Karunamayi, the smoke that rises from a homa, along with the vibrations of mantras chanted while various ingredients are offered into the sacred fire, contains a powerful healing energy that stimulates the cells of the brain and strengthens the nervous system. When these items burn, the fire releases subtle vibrations that have the power to destroy many kinds of pollution and purify the atmosphere. I enjoyed participating and being by the fire, because even though the smoke irritated my eyes, the minute I closed my eyes I entered a higher dimension quickly and nothing disturbed my meditative state.

Shaktipat

Along with meditation, bhakti yoga, and the rituals I've described, Amma talked about the benefits of *shaktipat*, which occurs during meditation when a guru places a hand on each participant's head and transmits her divine radiance to them. I had read so much about this that I was extremely eager to receive the transmission, for I knew that the guru can help cleanse our energy channels and clear any passage that is blocked. Because the guru's energy is purer and of a higher quality than ours, this action provides more pranic energy to our system. This in turn helps us to clear our own pathways much faster, allowing our inner energy to move toward the crown chakra at the top of the head. With shaktipat, Amma explained, one can attain Self-realization without years of continuous practice—provided, of course, that one is receptive and ready. And by *ready*, Amma meant simply that some people have accumulated merit from spiritual practices performed in their previous births and are already at an advanced evolutionary stage.

Normal mortal consciousness carries such a small amount of prana, which has a low vibrational frequency, that it is incapable of clearing all the blockages that have been accumulated for many lifetimes. The ego restricts the free-flowing life force from entering our system. What prana we do carry is being utilized for day-to-day activities of the body and mind. We normally have to meditate for many years to accumulate more prana, without which we can't elevate our self. And so, when the energy of the guru is transmitted into our body through shaktipat, it's like getting an enormous energy boost to awaken the dormant kundalini. Amma also emphasized the importance of pranayama, or breath control, before and after meditation, as it increases the intake of prana to the entire system. Pranayama is like having the key to open the door before we enter a room. Initially, we need to use this effective tool to control and calm the mind.

Prana

In India the name of the life force flowing and pulsating in all living things is *prana,* or *maha shakti* ("great energy"). It is also called *chi* or *ki* in Asia, as well as vital energy, bioenergy, cosmic energy, and primordial life energy. The conscious control of pranic energy activates and sustains life in the body. Before I learned differently, I used to think that what we breathe is oxygen, and that keeps us alive. But now I understand that when we breathe in air, we are taking in prana along with the oxygen, and that as we meditate the vital energy or life force increases tremendously. Prana, which literally means "breath" in Sanskrit, uses oxygen as a vehicle to distribute itself through the breath and blood to every part of the body, and that is what keeps us going. It is a vibration rather than a gross electrical energy, and how much of it we have makes a difference in how vibrant and full of life we feel. Raising the pranic frequency can change our perception and our level of power and improve our quality of life. When we have too many health problems, we end up having more prana outside the body than within. When we don't replace the loss of this energy for a prolonged period, we tend to suffer mentally or physically. According to ancient Vedic teachings, when we are unwell the quality of prana and its density within our system seem to be greatly reduced. The cause of pain or imbalance in our gross body is usually this reduction in pranic flow to a specific area. By giving a boost of that energy to a particular area and increasing the vibrational frequency, we can eliminate the discomfort or pain.

All this may sound simple enough, but it requires a tremendous amount of focus and concentration. Once I achieved this insight, I learned to put it into practice whenever it was needed. The power comes only after we reach certain depths in meditation by attaining complete stillness. I discovered that merely directing the movement of the vibrating energy with our mind to the particular chakra closest to the area of discomfort or pain and commanding it to raise the vibrational frequency could lead to healing. Soon after I would give the instruction to the command center (the ajna chakra, between the eyebrows), the vibration of the chakra involved would increase tremendously. Within a few minutes the pain would subside and harmonize the area that was causing the discomfort, providing balance to the entire gross body.

Pranayama is the conscious control of the flow of prana and so is beneficial not only for meditation but for our day-to-day existence. Whenever I am outdoors in the fresh air I take deep breaths and do pranayama for a few minutes so that I can accumulate more vital energy in my system. This practice gives me such an extra boost of vigor that it has become a daily habit. Meditation is essential to raising our consciousness, because it increases our supply of prana and we require high amounts of prana to achieve a higher energy field with a higher vibrational frequency. The higher the frequency, the closer we get to the Source.

Yogananda called prana—"sparks of intelligent finer-than-atomic energy that constitutes—life."[1] He distinguished two types of prana in this physical world: one that is a kind of cosmic vibratory energy everywhere in the universe structuring and sustaining all things; and a second form that pervades and sustains each human body. [2]

In his autobiography, *Living with Kundalini*, Gopi Krishna called it "an inseparable part of the cosmic energy or shakti that resides in all life. It is the driving force behind all cosmic phenomena." He also acknowledged that prana utilizes oxygen as a main vehicle for its activity, adding that it possesses "a super-human intelligence and memory beyond the range of our thought."

I have long felt that the strength of prana in us determines our level of consciousness, and that this level changes as we evolve. Any illness, disease, or overuse of drugs or intoxicants can change the proportion of consciousness within as it alters our pranic spectrum. From what I understand, each of us is a form of life energy that manifests its own particular spectrum of prana, which vibrates and expresses its being. This may be one reason people manifest so many different personalities, behavior patterns, intellectual levels, and temperaments. As John White points out, "Our human personality is an expression of single consciousness, just as the electromagnetic spectrum is a multiband expression of a single characteristic electromagnetic wave."[3]

Eckhart Tolle also speaks in terms of vibrational frequencies: "In the higher consciousness, the energy we emanate and that runs our life is of a much higher vibrational frequency than that of mind energy that everyone uses in lower limited conscious frequency."[4]

Swami Muktananda and others have pointed out that the shakti, or energy, of prana takes on five different forms to carry out the different functions of the body in an orderly manner. Each of the five forms has a different Sanskrit name: *Prana* is the breath. *Apana* expels waste matter from the body. *Samana* carries the nourishment of food to the part of the body where it is needed. *Vyana* fills the body as the power of movement that makes it function. And *Udana* resides in the the body's central channel and works upwards.

As we have seen, pranayama balances and controls our breathing, which greatly enhances our power of concentration during meditation. It also helps awaken inner energy that has been dormant and stirs up the entire nervous system, compelling it to produce an enhanced supply of pranic fuel for the brain. We can learn to regulate this energy within our body and its movement through our mind, and even target it to reach a specific location. Prana also helps us disconnect the mind from any thoughts, life functions, and sensory perceptions that tie us to body consciousness.

Once the mind becomes calm by itself after enough meditative practice, we no longer need to do pranayama. The mind then goes directly to the object of concentration without our wasting time trying to control the mind. In the early stages of my sadhana, I performed pranayama regularly. But as I went into deeper states of consciousness during my meditations, I did not use pranayama for that purpose. Still, in general I regard it as an important and helpful tool in every aspect in life. When I advanced to deeper states, I learned to end my meditation by doing pranayama prior to reverting to ordinary consciousness. As I took each breath, I could see the Divine shining with a bright golden sphere surrounding an opal-blue sphere. This is direct proof of pranic energy existing all around us and going into every breath we take. We can see this only after we have been meditating for some time.

Amma emphasized the need to maintain silence as much as possible throughout the retreat, as a great deal of vital energy gets lost while speaking. "Silence is the language of God," she likes to say, and being silent allows us to preserve that energy and dive deep into the self within during our meditation. Further, she says,

> Ignorant people argue too much,
>
> Intelligent people converse,
>
> Seers, the wise ones, live in the power of silence.

Devotion

Without devotion no growth or movement along the path is possible. It is both the essential prerequisite and the most integral aspect of our spiritual journey. But for me devotion does not mean sitting in front of sacred image and reciting chants and Sanskrit mantras, performing ritualistic activities, or visiting temples. All those forms of devotion may be suitable, and I have participated in a few of them myself. I have visited temples occasionally, as I have heard that many temples and idols can be inspiring and can have a positive vibrational impact on the visitor. Some places and certain sacred images that have been established for centuries are known to transmit an abundance of cosmic energy to those that visit them.

By and large, however, I have always had an intuitive regard for the inner self, because I know the Divine dwells within us. As Swami Muktananda stated, "Meditate on your Self. Honor your Self. Worship your Self. Understand your Self. God dwells within you as you."[5] I have always had great faith in and devotion to the Supreme Power that oversees this existence. I believe that experiencing the Truth directly by realization is more effective than worshipping its description in some material form. I have always believed in the Self, the Divine that dwells within each of us, as the Supreme Reality, which is probably why I was drawn to the inner journey of meditation as opposed to other methods. As I understand them, rituals and prayers in which one is seeking guidance or help from something "out there," known as the Supreme or God, imply that there is still duality—oneself and the object of worship—whereas meditation implies oneness that is already within us. Demanding that *something else* fix things may give us gratification or a temporary solution but can never really bring a full understanding of Truth or Reality.

Once we attain realization, duality falls away, but that can happen only when we lose all desires, demands, and cravings, even if for something as simple as peace of mind. And only meditation can lead us to that oneness so directly; other methods simply prepare us for knowing the truth. Long practice had accustomed me to sit in the same posture for hours without discomfort, so that I was able to continue my meditations with ease. Everything and everyone, including social life, food, daily chores, and entertainment, became secondary to my desire for self-knowledge. I became increasingly preoccupied with the mystery of Truth, and the weeks I spent with Amma at her retreat furthered and deepened that preoccupation.

Above all else, I came to understand that Self-realization is a progressive journey toward the Ultimate Reality at the core of our being. It is the direct perceptual experience by which we can identify our True Self, or soul, which amounts to the individualized reflection of God. During the retreat, Amma often addressed us as embodied divine souls, which is a more accurate and beautiful way of addressing us than by our names or occupations or any other identities generated by this egocentric existence. But instead of *being* embodied divine souls, we have altered ourselves and forgotten who we really are. Self-realization helps us remember and acknowledge that we are divine souls existing in physical bodies, and not merely the material beings we have *become*.

Increasing the Flow of Prana, or Vital Energy, to the Body

Normally our breathing is not even; our inhalations and exhalations are of different length and force. The main purpose of breath control, or pranayama, is to regulate the incoming and outgoing breath. To experience this, sit upright in a comfortable posture and begin by closing the right nostril and inhaling deeply through the left nostril. Then close the left nostril and exhale completely through the right. Keeping the left nostril closed, inhale deeply through the right; then close the right nostril and exhale completely through the left. That constitutes one round or cycle. Complete five rounds before beginning your meditation practice. Each cycle should take exactly the same amount of time so the mind can turn inward in meditation. With practice, this will greatly enhance the power of concentration during meditation.

Although this breath-control practice is ideal as a prelude to meditation, you can also use it any time of day. If you're feeling agitated or stressed out, angry or fatigued, take a few moments to go through these same five cycles of alternate-nostril breathing, and you will be astonished at the results.

SEVEN
Places I Felt Compelled to Visit

And then, before I realized it, the two-week retreat was over and the time had come to return home. Though I felt sad leaving Penusila Ashram and saying goodbye to Amma and to the place I never wanted to leave, I felt I was taking home something extremely valuable that would be of use continually. All spiritual teachers give their tools to their disciples, but how we make use of those tools and the knowledge they provide is up to each individual. How much effort we put into applying those tools makes all the difference in our progress. After observing many devotees in the ashram, I was astonished at how some of them place almost all their trust in these teachers. They seemed to be under the misconception that one automatically obtains liberation or enlightenment simply by spending time around enlightened teachers or holy people. Yet I became convinced that this kind of thinking will cause us to lose our own purpose and sense of the Divine within. Once we receive direction from the teacher, we need to find our own way.

I left with a positive attitude, full of energy and knowing exactly what I needed to do from that point forward. Everything was clear and I had a precisely planned-out road map toward the goal of Self-realization. Living and working for so many years in America, I had come to approach my spiritual quest with a bit of Western vigor, courage, and tenacity, determined to do whatever I needed to attain realization.

Among the things that had arisen within me when I returned was the drive to accomplish my task no matter what. My desire, devotion, and discipline had increased exponentially. During those two weeks with Karunamayi, I progressed more rapidly than in all the time I had spent working on my own during the past few years. That is the true value of an enlightened teacher—not simply to want to continue to be in her presence but to be inspired and energized to do the utmost in your own time.

After the retreat, I set out on a journey to visit the sacred places of India and to meet with other spiritual masters and teachers. At the same time, I was driven to seek out other individuals on the path to Self-realization, people I could listen to and spend time with. I felt comfortable with them because of our shared goal as well as a common desire to be with people on a similar level of consciousness. That's only natural, just as writers and artists like to associate with each other. And the reasons are similar: interacting socially with like-minded individuals who share your way of thinking and like the same kinds of activities helps reinforce your own desire to advance on one's chosen path.

I had heard about all manner of other holy places in India, where a variety of saints and sages had followed a path similar to the one I was on. I believed that the high vibrations exuded by the meditations of these spiritual masters still remained as they had been during their presence, and that anyone visiting there would benefit from being exposed to them. Some of the sages had spent many years in meditation, including great teachers of Advaita Vedanta, who described the spiritual realities of Self-realization and raised the overall consciousness of mankind. I decided to visit a few of the most renowned places and meet any of these holy teachers who were still alive. Once again, the places I would visit, when I would go, and what I would do all seem to have been preplanned by some guiding force that was directing my life.

Ramana Maharshi Ashram

I chose to start by visiting the Maharshi Ashram in Tiruvannamalai, followed by the Sri Aurobindo ashram in Pondicherry; Paramahansa Yogananda's ashram, Ranchi, in Calcutta; and one of Satya Sai Baba's ashrams. I also visited the holy city of Varanasi on the Ganges, a central locus of Indian spirituality; and Saranath, the birthplace of Buddhism. I had become aware that these holy places were located in areas that had a higher concentration of impoverished individuals, and so I went there not only to meditate, but also to involve myself with charitable service.

I visited Ramana Maharshi Ashram mostly to spend quality time meditating around Arunachala Mountain. When I reached Tiruvannamalai, I asked to see the two caves in particular where Ramana had spent much of his life, Skanda Ashram and Virupaksha Cave. In those caves the sage of Arunachala lived for twenty-two years, blessed devotees, and benefited all mankind spiritually. Climbing up the mountain to those caves was an arduous task. Though steps led up to the caves, the steep inclination proved surprisingly strenuous, and the scorching heat made this trek even more taxing than I had anticipated. It took me close to an hour to go up and another to return, as I needed to take occasional breaks from the intense heat. Despite all of this, on the way up I appreciated how beautiful the surrounding greenery was. It was like walking through a forest, which in essence I was. Farther up the mountain, monkeys darted out of the woods. At first I was apprehensive, as I did not know what they were doing,

Ramana Maharshi

Sarada at the Ramana Maharshi Ashram

and proceeded with my climb a tad wary of what was behind me. Once I turned around, though, I noticed a couple of monkeys coming up the mountain with me as if they were my companions on the path.

I can barely describe how wonderful I felt after entering the cave. An energetic force suffused me and made it easy to succeed in climbing all the way up, filling me with immense satisfaction and happiness. Once I reached the top, it was easy to get into a meditative state and forget all the difficulties I had faced on the climb. I had heard that thousands of devotees from all over the world came to this spot to deepen their meditations.

Tiruvannamalai is also one of the great temple towns of South India, sitting right at the base of Arunachala Mountain, which is said to represent the physical manifestation of Lord Shiva. A kind of spiritual vortex, it contains numerous ashrams and temples, and although it's not the sort of place I would have visited under normal circumstances, I believed that I had been brought there for a purpose. It felt like visiting a place of enormous significance for so many people, and I spent one week going up and down the mountain and many hours meditating. I got up early each morning and ate a little something to sustain myself, then spent almost the entire day on the mountain. I did not think of coming down until I had finished at least four or five hours of meditation, taking only short breaks.

Those hours of meditation did not feel long at all, as I went into samadhi rapidly. One time the person in charge of the cave had to come and wake me from my meditation to let me know that the place was closing for the night. As I was leaving he mentioned that he had tried calling to me, and when I did not respond he finally tapped my shoulder to let me know it was time for me to leave. He also warned me to be careful going down the hill to the ashram, saying it wasn't good for women to walk alone in the forest, but to go with a group. I thought it was kind of him to do so; however, I was not worried, as I had become familiar with the terrain from my daily visits.

On another day the sun was setting while I was coming down from the cave, so I decided to situate myself and enjoy the beautiful vista from the top of the hill, where I could see the whole city. Reveling in the change of colors as the sun sank in the sky, I gently closed my eyelids, appreciating the natural loveliness of my surroundings. Suddenly I was in deep samadhi, unaware of where I was. As my intention had been to watch the sun set, I tried to open my eyes. Suddenly I observed not only the brightness of the sunset, but also how all the surroundings were scintillating, as if they had been sprinkled with the glitter of energy everywhere. All the trees, every little shrub, every small plant with flowers, and every piece of matter was shining with such brightness that all I could see was their glow. I was so astonished that I truly did not know where I was for that moment and became totally disoriented. So I closed my eyes once again, not able to believe whether what I saw was real or a dreamscape. Surely for that moment

I had entered a different dimension of my consciousness—one that I would never forget, as such glowing beauty could be seen only in an expanded state of consciousness. Finally, after some time, I came out of my meditation and noticed that it was getting dark, so I started walking back down the hill. After Amma's ashram, the ashram and caves at Arunachala Mountain became my second-favorite place to practice my meditation.

My next visit was to the city of Varanasi on the Ganges, the holiest river in India, which originates up on Mount Kailash and flows through the north, into the Bay of Bengal near Kolkatta (Calcutta). Varanasi is one of the oldest continuously inhabited cities in the world (the oldest in India), and the banks of the Ganges have been the site of centuries of meditation by many God-realized saints. Along the river are many *ghats*—Sanskrit for "steps" or "landings." Varanasi alone has nearly a hundred ghats that lead to the Ganges. Although some claim that the river is polluted due to daily ablutions performed by Hindus to purify themselves, I have been told that a back current on the surface of the water flowing north helps the river to process waste.

The banks of India's most sacred river,
The Ganges at Varanasi

I could feel something special about the place, a powerful energy that may have sprung in part from the vast numbers of people who come there toward end of their lives to die so that they can be cremated on the Ganges as a final purification. Though I did not stay there for long, I managed to take a boat ride toward the center of the river and felt the soothing effect—a consoling, pleasant feeling—while I was in the water. I have fond memories of watching the sunrise early in the morning as everyone was bathing in the river. I did meditate for a while, but I could not stay long, as the river was always crowded with bathers and people performing rituals and I felt a bit overwhelmed.

Saranath

From Varanasi it was a journey of just a few miles to Saranath, considered to be the birthplace of Buddhism: the deer park where the Buddha first taught after he became enlightened, and where the Buddhist *sangha*, or community, came into existence. I wanted to see the stupa and the

The Bodhi Tree,
where The Buddha attained enlightenment.

The Buddha in reclining position, depicting the last time he laid down before dying and entering nirvana.

statue of the Buddha lying down that have been erected there, but mostly I wanted to see the Bodhi tree that is said to be a descendent of the original tree under which the Buddha became enlightened, in Bodh Gaya, which was just a few hours by car from Saranath. I was fascinated to see that the shape of the tree resembled an umbrella under which one could easily sit for a deep meditation. The tree provided such cool shade that I myself wanted to sit under it, but the large number of other visitors appreciating the site kept me from staying longer.

Pondicherry

The Sri Aurobindo Ashram is located in the town of Pondicherry, on the southeastern coast of India. A town with a rich French influence, it is right on the ocean and contains a beautiful garden between the main building and the ocean. This was the home of Sri Aurobindo, who was both a revolutionary for India's independence and one of its most influential gurus in the first half of the twentieth century. Once the basic needs of food, shelter, and clothing have been taken care of, Aurobindo believed, humans can strive to achieve their full potential by meditation, contemplation, and yoga, which is how he began his own spiritual journey. Further, for all the higher practices of spirituality to be effective, he taught, our inner energy must be awakened. Only then can we practice genuine yoga and have real transformation take place. I visited both Pondicherry and Auroville, where he created a perfect ambience to achieve higher states of consciousness. I wanted to see the place where Sri Aurobindo entered samadhi, and spent some time there meditating and paying my respects to those divine souls who guided so many on the spiritual path. This was also where his spiritual collaborator of Sri Aurobindo, a French woman, mystic, and occultist called "the Mother," lived and taught. It was a white marble tomb overshadowed by a large tree and almost completely covered in flowers, which created the most wonderful fragrance.

At the Sri Aurobindo Ashram. A hall that honors spiritual teachers from different lineages.

Sri Aurobindo and The Mother

Although this place brought inner tranquility, the aura of peace around the tomb site was of a different nature, much as when I visited Maharshi's ashram. As I approached the tomb of those two great souls, I could feel a pressure vibrating in my forehead and my ajna chakra. My meditations there were effortless and extremely deep, and I felt as if there was an alignment of our two energy fields and a communication between them. Once again I left with a feeling of joy.

Encinitas

Paramahansa Yogananda walking the grounds at the Encinitas Hermitage, Retreat & Gardens in Encinitas in the 1930s.

My next visit was to the Encinitas Hermitage, Retreat & Gardens in California where Paramahansa Yogananda lived for many years and began the first Self-Realization Fellowship. It is situated high above the Pacific Ocean, and the first time I saw it I felt so soothed and refreshed with the spectacular view that I felt invited to be part of it. The peace and silence were so extraordinary that I was drawn to meditating there. Yogananda taught a system of powerful scientific meditation techniques for attaining direct personal experience of

God realization through a part of the science of kriya yoga, which he presented in his book *Autobiography of a Yogi.* The system consists of levels of pranayama based on techniques that are intended to rapidly accelerate spiritual development and lead to union of the soul with God. His teachings emphasized the value of self-effort in changing our limited mortal consciousness into God Consciousness.

Sarada in reflection at the beach below the Encinitas Hermitage

The beautiful meditation gardens at the Encinitas Hermitage

Yogananda established many Self-Realization Fellowship temples and meditation centers throughout the world, emphasizing the one divine highway to which all paths of religious beliefs eventually lead, bringing all of us to devotion to God. He introduced hundreds of thousands of truth-seekers to the ancient science and philosophy of Yoga and its universally applicable methods of meditation, but more than anything he advocated cultural and spiritual understanding between East and West, and the exchange of their finest distinctive features. "I am not interested in crowds," he said, "but in souls who are in earnest to know God."[1]

Puttaparthi

The ashrams and sacred sites I had visited before now were all places whose founders had passed away some years before. But the great modern sage Sathya Sai Baba was still living at that time and I wanted to have his *darshan*, or blessing. Sai Baba was in a wheelchair because of his fractured hip, but I was happy to meet him under any circumstances, as his teachings emphasized the highest ideals of truth, right conduct, peace, love, and nonviolence. He encouraged us to see that we are not our mind and not our body, and to recognize who we truly are—the eternal spirit that temporarily occupies this mind and body. We can appreciate and become who we really are, he said, by turning inward with faith in God and an intense yearning to know him. To Sai Baba, our conscience is a reflection of the eternal spirit of God; his mission was to motivate love for God and service to humankind. I'm glad that I had a chance to see him then, as he passed away a few years later.

Sathya Sai Baba

Some believe that Sai Baba was an avatar, which traditionally means an incarnation of God on earth. Christians, for instance, believe that

Jesus was the avatar of God the Father, just as Hindus believe that Krishna was an avatar of the god Vishnu (who had other avatars as well). I believe that an avatar is anyone who attains union with Divine Spirit and then returns to earth to help humankind. These souls carry the highest manifestations of the Divine and can bring a great forward movement to humankind's spiritual evolution. They may also provide a kind of drastic medicine to destroy the evil toxins in humanity, give a boost to the evolution of human consciousness, establish virtues, and save the good. These avatars come with a specific purpose and acquire a few earnest disciples who help them fulfill their needs while they are in this human embodiment. I also believe that at times they may expose their full powers to those who work closely with them, in order to gain their confidence and faith. Among the signs of avatars are *siddhis*, or supernatural powers, including the ability to transform energy into matter and matter into energy. Sai Baba was believed to be able to manifest matter, including sacred ash, called *vibhuti*, which he distributed to those who came to his ashram.

However, in part because of Sai Baba's confinement to a wheelchair and the enormous size of the crowds that came to his ashram, I wasn't able even to attempt to approach him for a personal meeting. As he was wheeled down the aisles of the huge hall in which he appeared, I was able to make brief eye contact, but that was the extent of it. Nonetheless, I was happy to have gone to visit Sai Baba's ashram and to catch even a glimpse of the holy man.

After completing my pilgrimages to the sites of these great sages, I attended several conferences and philosophical talks on the nature of consciousness. I was thrilled to see so many scientists and philosophers able to assimilate different approaches regarding the issue of consciousness from disciplines including philosophy, cognitive science, neuroscience, and medicine. Each contributed input to move toward an integrated understanding of human consciousness and how consciousness is generated. For instance, those reflecting an Eastern outlook believe that consciousness is beyond scientific computation and that we need to experience it directly. I also attended several workshops and talks on nondualism, a generic name for the Advaita Vedanta beliefs of my teacher, Amma. Nonduality refers to the essential unity of all Being, and maintains that appearances to the contrary are merely illusion. As we have entered the age of quantum physics, which acknowledges that matter and energy are essentially different manifestations of the same reality, modern science has grown closer in spirit to the wisdom of the great avatars and teachers of the East.

EIGHT

Self-Discipline: Diet, Exercise, and Training the Mind

Based on my experience in the ashram and being with Sri Karunamayi, whom I now considered my teacher, and my pilgrimage to other holy places, I had learned what I would need to do to reach ultimate union with Universal Consciousness. More than anything else, the journey would require stringent self-discipline, comprising the divine intuitive power to do the right thing at the right time. Our intuitive voice constantly sends us valuable information regarding what to eat, what to say, how much to exercise, how long we should rest, and what kinds of friendships we need to form. All we have to do is listen to our inner voice without fail. The human is the only form in which we can directly experience the shift toward higher consciousness. We are the only embodied beings that are capable of raising ourselves to a higher plane. As sages have said, we are not human beings having a spiritual experience, but spiritual beings having a human experience.

One further insight became clear to me as I learned about the great variety of techniques and practices to raise our spiritual consciousness, and the many paths followed by great masters such as Yogananda, Ramana Maharshi, and Nisargadatta Maharaj: Whatever path one chooses requires tremendous effort and commitment. And to keep that commitment, we need to exert will power and let go of attachment to certain things that may be tempting, whether they are simple pleasures or the natural human inclination to waste time. The upside of that commitment as I came to understand it, though, is that whatever we do willingly will attract more cosmic energy into our body. What I said in the previous chapter about how meditation and deep breathing bring more pranic energy into our system also applies to exercising will. I believe that any action that activates or stimulates our will power brings in more energy so that we can accomplish our goals more easily. Without applying our will power, we cannot move forward on the spiritual path.

You don't need to withdraw from life's active pursuits or be like Sri Ramakrishna, Yogananda, Swami Muktananda, or Ramana Maharshi—Indian saints who left their homes to go into seclusion for a time before emerging to teach thousands of followers. You don't need to spend years practicing austerities, setting up ashrams, or writing books. Each of these men was just like us, except perhaps that his destiny led him to take that route. At the same time, it's important to understand that we cannot actively pursue Self-realization if we are not ready. Certain life situations may not allow us to follow this path—for example, the responsibilities of raising children or the need to devote most of our time to earning a living. Forcing something at the wrong time in our life can be counterproductive. Eventually, though, the appropriate circumstances and opportunity will lead us into that divine calling in a way that allows us to follow through. In the meantime, yoga, meditation, or any form of spiritual discipline will definitely lead to a higher level of spiritual growth.

Having grasped this principle, I decided to be much more disciplined with regard to my health and pay closer attention to the food I ate, how I exercised, and how much rest I got, as well as to the training of my mind. I put much emphasis on maintaining good health. I knew it would give me greater capacity and strength and would make it much easier for me to attain the goal as well as to fulfill all my other responsibilities. To allow the mind to be free to meditate and to focus on the spiritual path requires disciplining the body continually—in a sense, attaining good spiritual health just as an athlete trains to reach peak physical condition. Accordingly, I set out on a path of discipline that included yoga, mind training, and a diet that would allow me to spend my energy on spiritual practice instead of digestion and so on. These three disciplines are all interrelated. We have to train the mind to withdraw our attention from all objects of distraction and place it consistently on only one area. In a sense, the less you feed the mind, the more room you have to fill it with the energy needed to engage in long-term, intensive meditation. Likewise, we need to maintain a high level of overall health and psychological integration so the body and mind can pursue the deeper aspects of yoga.

The Dalai Lama has made the point that we often sacrifice health to make more money and then have to spend money to regain our health! He also said that we are so anxious about the future that we can't enjoy the present. If we want to live to our full potential at each moment, we need to care for our health from the outset, so that it becomes second nature to take care of the divine vessel through which we experience our soul. We experience the Truth only through our body. For consciousness to manifest, it needs the body as a vehicle, one that must be taken care of and given the right kind of fuel. We reach higher consciousness most quickly and effectively through controlled discipline and the daily practice of meditation. But for this to occur we must give meditation preference over all other activities and develop what I call the three Ds: desire, devotion, and discipline. Of course, without sincerity, patience, faith, will power, and a craving to know the Truth we will not be able to move forward.

We tend to take our body and health for granted, without realizing the body's intrinsic value as a perfect vehicle for being in contact with God and for fully experiencing Divine Consciousness. Maintaining a healthy, serene body brings a freedom that we aren't aware of until it is no longer there. We use the body for hedonistic ends or for expressing our vanity, through many lifetimes. Our focus ought to be on using our body to gain experience and learn the lessons we need to learn in each life. This way we can evolve and end the cycle of embodiment.

Diet

For some reason, even when I was young I seemed to have good eating habits and didn't indulge in food that was not right for my body. It is as though something inside me was telling me to eat right and take care of my physical being for a bigger purpose. For that reason, perhaps, my body had already been preparing itself for the long journey I was embarking on.

A weak or sickly body will not be able to tolerate the process of purification you need to go through, so when you embark on the journey you have to be very motivated to pursue a strict diet. Good health does not come all of a sudden, but from conscious and continuous effort and listening to your finely tuned inner system. Some people may say, "You are lucky that you have good health," or "God gave you good health," but I don't think luck has anything to do with it. I believe that, as Ben Franklin once said, God helps those who help themselves, and this is as true of our health as it is of attaining Self-realization. Once God gives us the indication that we are ready, it is up to us to make the effort and to be able to follow the path to the end. Divine intervention definitely plays a role, but we are still responsible for paying attention to the signs God gives us and then putting in the effort.

You cannot govern your eating habits, for example, by what pleases your senses. You have to be continuously aware of what goes into your system and make sure your diet contains the principal components of food—protein, carbohydrates, and good fats—in proper proportion, consumed at appropriate intervals. In my case I ate mostly sattvic (or pure) vegetarian items freshly prepared just before eating. I was also aware of the importance of avoiding foods that cause sleepiness and laziness. Being vegetarian was not based on any custom, religious belief, or moral principles. I ate that way solely because it felt right for my particular system and the way my inner organs work. Our organs require energy to digest and process food, and it's better to give the system less work by eating right and limiting portions. We should be conserving energy for a higher purpose.

I have heard that eating food that has been stored in the refrigerator for several days is not good for the system, because older food loses some of its nutritional benefit. The food we eat should be prepared just before we consume it. There is a misconception that protein comes solely from meat and other flesh foods, but one can meet the dietary requirements for protein with vegetarian items, such as lentils, legumes, sprouts, and nuts. According to some spiritual teachers, eating meat, such as beef and pork, can be harmful to the nervous system, creating overstimulation and even aggressiveness. If you pay attention to how you feel after eating certain foods, you may discover that your body does not require as much protein as everyone seems to think. Eat plenty of fresh fruit, green and yellow vegetables, grains, legumes, nuts, and dairy, including milk, buttermilk, yogurt, and cottage cheese. Always be careful to drink plenty of water and fresh juice, whether you are thirsty or not. I drink at least eight glasses of water every day because I know my system requires it. Water aids in digestion, absorbs and metabolizes nutrients, and keeps the body hydrated so that it functions properly.

The key to good health is not to overeat or under eat, yet to keep the stomach empty as much as possible. Food intake should be directly proportional to your level of activity; otherwise you will create health problems. The best rule of thumb is to eat only when hungry. Make sure the food you eat is easily digestible and takes little energy to process. At times it can be difficult to attend to this aspect and get that perfect balance. Starving or avoiding certain food groups can do more harm than good, so you need to learn to maintain balance in your diet whether or not you feel hungry. For example, if I missed any of the four food groups in my daily consumption, I would make sure to eat what I missed. If I didn't eat fruit in one of my meals, for example, I would be careful to include it in my next meal and do without something else to make up.

The quality and quantity of the food you consume should be your main concern. Green vegetables, for instance, have a high density of nutrients and relatively few calories, compared to many other foods. Further, your inner being will dictate what and when to eat. Always pay attention to what type of food your inner self asks for, what your soul demands, and what best suits your constitution, while not succumbing to negative temptations. Although I was tempted at times to indulge myself with food that was not right for my stomach, I usually didn't give in, because showing discipline with food was very important to me. The energy of the body is of the Divine and we must value it, since we experience everything through it. We must treat the body in a divine manner. As Jack Kornfield writes in *After the Ecstasy, The Laundry,* "Enlightenment must be lived here and now through this very body or else it is not genuine. Embodied enlightenment is about living wisely in our particular body, as it is, on this day, in this amazing life."[1]

When you believe in taking good care of the body and mind, you will be less tempted to indulge in extreme behavior of any kind; moderation will be the key. I have heard that one must already be in a higher spectrum of consciousness, carrying a higher energy field, to have the yearning to maintain good health and to be able to apply these principles of life; but even then this discipline does not come easily. Raising your vibrational frequency generates a higher level of thought and reinforces positive perceptions. "Health is a state of complete harmony of the body, mind and spirit," says the yoga master B. K. S. Iyengar: "Evolution includes all aspects of one's being, from bodily health to Self-realization."[2] So I have often wondered why many renowned spiritual teachers suffered from bad health. Enlightened beings including Ramana Maharshi, Sri Ramakrishna, and J. Krishnamurti have died of cancer, and others may have suffered unnecessarily from poor health and emotional problems during their years of spiritual practice. For reasons I cannot fathom, maintaining good health has not always been among their priorities.

Suffice it to say that unless we are fully aware of the multiplicity of elements within the body, we will be more prone to illnesses and suffering. As the Mother puts it in her *Commentaries on the Divine Life,* "No significant dimension can be excluded and left unconscious from awareness until all the cells, organs, and the way they function are in harmony."[3] To be sure, some spiritual teachers and yoga masters have lived to be a hundred years old, and the Buddha himself is believed to have died at about the age of eighty in an era when life expectancy was half that, so I can't say why other great adepts died younger or suffered painful ailments. But this I do believe, as it was put so well by Mahatma Gandhi in his self-published newspaper, *Young India*: "One cannot do right in one department of life while still occupied in doing wrong in any other department. Life is an indivisible whole."[4]

Exercise

We all know how important exercise is in our daily lives, but to paraphrase a famous slogan, *Just Don't Overdo It.* Some individuals believe that to reach their full fitness potential they must overexert themselves while exercising. However, I believe that exercise should be done only to the extent needed to tone our body, not to exhaust us. Each body is structured to accommodate its limits, and any workout should be done accordingly. Some people constantly push themselves beyond their limits, believing that they will achieve further benefit. But you can reach a point of diminishing returns. It is important to get physical exercise in order to improve the overall functioning of the body and to allow our energy to flow freely throughout the body, but even a simple walk may be as beneficial as a vigorous one-hour run. It invigorates the system with freshness, helping the body to take in sufficient oxygen. To determine which exercise is best for you, all you have to do is listen to your body's cues. Certain yoga asanas, or postures, are better at times because they tone, balance, and strengthen us without agitating the whole system. In the end, the person who practices yoga or takes a light stroll may be just as healthy as one who leaves the gym in a pool of sweat. To attain an overall state of well-being, there is no need to struggle.

The right level of physical exercise should leave your body refreshed and more able to sit in meditation for as long as you need. Meditation is a form of exercise for the mind and prevents mental aging and mental fatigue. To function optimally, you have to constantly stimulate your mind with new challenges; combining light physical exercise with meditation gives you the best of both worlds.

Rest

Because meditation demands a healthy body and a healthy mind, we must rest our body properly so that it can withstand the impact of intensive meditation. Sufficient sleep is just as important as proper food and exercise for maintaining health and overall quality of life. It allows our inner energy to flow freely through us and realign with its Source. We need sleep, especially deep sleep, with its involuntary relaxation of energy from the motor and sensory nerves, for energy renewal, which allows us to function in our day-to-day life. But we also need deep, worriless sleep to allow our True Self to return to its primordial state, in which it gets revitalized for the next day's work. One reason we feel so refreshed after having a good sleep is that it is only during sleep that our mortal consciousness unites with Cosmic Consciousness. The deep-sleep state is a reminder of what is beyond ordinary awareness: being in contact with our true nature. I will have more to say about this in the next chapter.

I don't place any importance on popular beliefs and advice regarding when to go to bed and when to wake up or exactly how much sleep we need. Although most medical sources say we should get at least seven hours a day, I don't believe there is one optimal amount of time, because it's an individual concern. In my experience, it never mattered if I got three hours or ten hours as long as we do not oversleep and become tamasic. Being well rested was all that mattered for me, and that's still true. But everyone is different, and depending on your workload or level of activity, you may need more or less sleep. The best way to get into a deep sleep cycle is to keep your bedroom dark and cool and avoid any stimulants before bedtime, which tend to interrupt the REM sleep periods that allow us to dream.

Focusing the Mind

Meditation was not an easy task for me at first. I had to work diligently to control my mind because, as with most people, my mind can get lazy at times. Indeed, the mind is like a spoiled little child with a short attention span that needs discipline and training. Children often cannot sit still in one place for a long time, and the mind is equally unable to stay with one thought; it flits from one thing to another, a tendency known as "monkey mind."

You can train yourself to keep your focus on the spot between the eyebrows all through your meditation. That spot, sometimes called the third eye or Christ consciousness, is the center of will and concentration. The Hindu scriptures call it *kutastha chaitanya,* and today it is sometimes called "witness consciousness," the ability to stand back and observe one's thoughts and actions with complete equanimity. Buddhists call this point between the eyebrows "calm abiding," meaning the place where mind overcomes distractions by external objects and continuously turns toward the one-pointed object.

The only way to accomplish this level of stillness is to train the mind repeatedly to stay in one place with one thought. The mind is easily distracted by almost anything, from a simple noise to something you may have watched on television, or even awareness of pending tasks. That is why, as I noted earlier, I used to take care of all my household chores or responsibilities before meditating. So, if you are willing to try this, make sure you've taken care of any pressing duties or work-related obligations, at least for the next few hours. Choose the point where you want to focus your attention, whether it's the third eye, the navel, or some sacred image on a table in front of you. Breathe in and out as described at the end of chapter 2, but with each breath direct your attention to the spot you have chosen. Don't try to "do" anything, but if your attention wanders, gently return it to the spot without criticizing yourself for losing focus.

Training the mind produces a positive transformation, eliminating the mind's defective qualities while improving those that are desirable. What we invoke from within ourselves makes a difference, so we should consciously try to generate and entertain good thoughts, as they lift us into a higher level of being. Just as we provide good nutrition for our physical body, so we should nourish the mind and keep our senses sharp with positive sensory impressions created through natural means. Outdoor activities, such as spending time in the countryside amid gardens or trees or ocean views, have a soothing impact on the mind. You should be careful not to accumulate mental "junk," which is any damaging sensory input, ranging from negative television programs, mindless socializing, and idle gossip to destructive habits. Any disturbance in the mental equilibrium will affect your composure, which is required for your meditation practice. Hence, we have to generate thoughts that are of higher quality and that don't dull the mind in the way that bad food harms the body. The company you keep also affects the kinds of thoughts you generate; you may know the biblical saying, "As a man thinks, so he is."

Whenever I am stuck indoors for an extended period of time, I begin to get agitated and restless. When we spend too much time with man-made entertainment, as opposed to being in nature, the mind's space perception becomes narrow and we may easily become anxious, even frantic. Any excessive stimulation of the senses or continuous excitement will cause disturbances in our nervous system. The natural environment will give strength to our character by generating positive thoughts. Being close to green surroundings clears the mind and gives peace and contentment by creating room for things that are of more value.

As you become more acutely aware of this, you may want to reduce your indulgence in superfluous aspects of life. For instance, when we are persistently engrossed in attending social activities, we expend a good deal of mental energy thinking about them in advance, deciding what to wear, who will be present, and how we will get there and back. Our energy is continuously directed to those matters, leaving less time and energy for meditation. Far from being the passive activity that some perceive it to be, meditation requires lots of energy. You must be strong and exercise a good deal of patience and tolerance to cope with constant distractions, so it helps to minimize what the mind has to think about.

In my case, I eventually eliminated any sort of unnecessary activities and appointments, reduced my social life, and had to give up many things I used to enjoy. Although I had already let go of some of these activities during my initial period of renunciation, I continued to drop others to make room for serious meditation. As a result, I was slow to keep up–to-date with the latest technologies, including smartphones, new computer software, and other gadgets. I felt that if I were to involve myself with the plethora of technological advances, I would be spending more time learning how to use them and keeping up-to-date than on meditation. Using my time efficiently was my first priority. This doesn't mean you can't use these devices, which are part of contemporary culture and communication.

Maintaining Health (Continuous Care of the Instrument)

Especially in the West, but also surprisingly in Eastern religious cultures, we are often taught that spirit is good and matter is bad, that the body and physical needs represent a lower form of consciousness. The irony is that without taking proper care of the body and maintaining good physical health, we won't be able to lead a spiritual life. To meditate, do deep breathing, or carry out any other spiritual task requires good health and stamina.

Apart from what I have already said in this chapter, there are no simple guidelines that I can give that will cover everything you need to do to stay healthy. But I can urge you to listen to your inner self and take good care of all aspects of the instrument that the Divine has provided you with. As Patanjali implied, physical and spiritual health are synergistic; each one supports the other. Doing spiritual practices to elevate your consciousness will help your body stay sound, and maintaining strength and stamina will allow your body to tolerate the rigors of spiritual practices, especially intensive meditation. Don't make the mistake of thinking that you are being spiritual by denying the body food, drink, or rest. Just the opposite is true. We have to make our body a perfect instrument, in which our metabolic processes and bodily rhythms work in total harmony.

Isn't that how a truly enlightened consciousness should work?

NINE
Why Meditate?

Some people find the idea of meditation pleasant or soothing, while others seem almost frightened of it and have much trouble sitting quietly, even for few minutes. And yet we all meditate to a certain extent when we focus our concentration to perform a certain task with our limited consciousness, whether it's repairing an engine, helping our child with homework, or just screwing in a lightbulb. Without a certain amount of one-pointed concentration, we wouldn't be able to do anything effectively. The concentration we use in deep meditation is different, however. Intensive concentration that frees the attention from all distractions to focus on one thought, or no thought, is the highest and most difficult type of focus. It may be a painful process as we ascend the many stages on the way. My teacher likes to say that "meditation is the hardest and highest form of spirituality." But if we meditate deeply on a daily basis, we awaken the blissful, immortal consciousness of God that is always within us, hidden in our innermost core.

Interest in meditation has been spreading exponentially in the decades since Maharishi Mahesh Yogi came to prominence by teaching meditation to celebrities including the Beatles. To cite just one more recent example, the renowned film director David Lynch, who has been practicing meditation for forty years, has announced that he hopes to teach meditation to the world and, as a result, create world peace.[1] Lynch had been inspired by Maharishi's teaching that meditation isn't just for monks and yogis but for the masses. But the practice still requires a level of will power, intention, and sincerity on the part of the practitioner. Meditation is a *conscious* process that puts us directly in touch with our true nature, or soul. Without conscious awareness, it is not meditation. Some people may imagine that meditation means just sitting, spacing out, and going into trance—or alternatively, trying to suppress our thoughts with force and effort. There may be some effort involved, but it must be a kind of effortless effort, a process that requires focus, not force.

In meditation we attain a conscious awareness of our inner Divinity; it is like being awake during deep sleep. As we experience our soul, or true nature, there is a conscious relaxation of the vital energy within all our bodily organs. When this happens we consciously raise our inner life energy to the highest chakra, at the crown of the head, and experience our soul merging with the universal consciousness and leaving the mortal sensory plane for a time. That's another way of saying that we bring our mortal consciousness to unite with Cosmic Consciousness—and do it consciously. Eventually we abide as that Primordial Consciousness, withdrawing our sensory consciousness from identification with the body by stilling the restless sensory mind.

We are also in contact with our True Self, or soul, while we are in deep sleep, as the soul leaves the body and gets rejuvenated as it yearns for freedom and limitless joy. This is why we often awake with a feeling of having had a "good rest" and may even recall fleeting memories of having been in a blissful state. But because we have been asleep, we have no conscious memory of our True Self. We do need at least the subconscious contact with the soul that is provided by sleep in order to forget, for a time, all the desires, sensations, and attachments we experience in waking life. Otherwise, we would become like an overworked machine, no longer able to keep going.

By contrast, in meditation we are immersed in our Self while remaining conscious. That conscious awareness is what lifts us to a higher level. Do you ever wonder why we constantly indulge ourselves in choosing extreme activities that give us thrills or excitement? Certain types of sports, for example, like skydiving and bungee jumping, induce a "rush" of adrenalin and good feelings, as do some drugs. Even sex takes us to that moment of extreme pleasure that allows us to experience that spark of ecstasy or bliss and attain the utmost euphoric state of awareness—at least for that particular moment. We are continuously seeking to experience the blissful glimpse of that nondual state of oneness, or contact with our soul, without even realizing that is what we are seeking. If such a brief glimpse can give us that much fulfillment and contentment, imagine how much more peace we can attain through experiencing the Truth.

Meditation is the activity through which we will experience that real joy or peace in a lasting way, whereas extreme sports, drugs, and sexual love bring only fleeting moments of bliss, which in some cases have unpleasant side effects. Another example of experiencing the bliss of oneness would be when we are dreaming. Have you ever awoken from a dreamlike state feeling filled with bliss and joy? The great teachers believe that this state of bliss that occurs during deep sleep is our natural state, but that we aren't aware of it because we are unconscious. And yet every so often we wake up still immersed in a deep sense of bliss that persists for a few moments. We feel that we have been in some ecstatic place to which we would give anything to return. If this has happened to you, whether in the morning or the middle of the night, you probably didn't want to get up but would have preferred to go back to sleep and reenter that state of blissful consciousness. Sometimes we may have a fleeting memory of dream content—sensations of flying or of being in a location of overwhelming physical beauty or with a particular individual. But more often we are simply left with a powerful sensation of completely ecstatic happiness. Above all was the sense of transcendent bliss, a sense that life could not be better or consciousness higher.

The discipline of daily pranayama (the breath-control exercises described in previous chapters) prior to meditation, proper and limited food, exercise, rest, and training the mind enable your spiritual development to progress with ease. Of these, pranayama is the most important tool—said to be the very key that unlocks the door—for meditation. After leaving my job, I was able to devote myself more extensively to my daily practice, with the result that my will power, intent, and sincerity increased tremendously. Amma had put emphasis on rising along with the sun, when the cosmic energy is at its highest peak. As I mentioned earlier, I had not felt compelled to meditate so early in the morning, but my faith in Amma's teachings was such that I wanted to take advantage of her guidance. At first, it was not an easy feat to rise at such an early hour and meditate for several hours at a time, but eventually I became accustomed to it.

Trying to silence the mind by force will always have a negative impact on the entire system, demeaning the purpose of meditation itself. Eliminating thoughts by constant struggle will not work, anyway. The natural tendency of our thoughts is to go everywhere continuously, but the solution is to learn to ignore them and stop putting so much emphasis on getting the mind to go completely blank. That will not help; the constant effort will drain our energy and take up much of our time. The trick is to achieve our goal regardless of the thoughts and be aware of everything that happens, without struggle. Ignoring something tends to make it assume less importance; this is true with everything in life.

Attempting to meditate with force or strain will not lead us to Truth. In genuine meditation, the clarity and understanding that arises from quietude appears on its own without being forced. With continuous practice, meditation leads to contemplation. Actually, according to some mystics, there is a difference between meditation and contemplation: meditation is the means, and contemplation is the end result; one is the path and the other is the end of the path. As I have experienced it myself, this turns out to be true. During meditation thoughts do arise, but eventually they are silenced as we end up contemplating the Truth.

The conscious effort to empty the mind or block out thoughts, or to choose a particular method of meditation will not lead to silence. It will merely mislead you into thinking you are meditating, when in reality you are not. Any calmness that results from such efforts is only a state of mind that is dull and numb, which mimics quietness. As a result you get nowhere and falsely continue to do so with no concrete advancement toward the goal. That genuine peace or tranquility is not something that you can generate by force through your mind. In true meditation the quietness that arises is spontaneous and natural; it feels as if the Divine is inviting you. No physical compulsion induces this invitation. Further, there is a set purpose and process to meditation, along with a definite goal.

Daily meditation has many physical benefits, including lowered blood pressure and pulse rate. It can also improve mental health, specifically in the prevention of some cognitive disorders, such as Alzheimer's disease, and reduce anxiety and depression. The deep, regulated breathing of pranayama accounts for some of the benefits, but on a basic level meditation allows us to be in our natural state and attain a balanced state of mind without any fluctuations or agitation. Although meditation does not take everyone to enlightenment, it does remodel our life and elevate us to higher consciousness, purifying our inner self in a way that makes it easier to control negative impulses, such as anger, jealousy, lust, and hatred. Daily meditation with sincerity will also help us develop the virtues of patience, compassion, and forgiveness, among others.

I also believe that meditation affects the aging process, because how young and vibrant one feels is simply a state of mind and an expression of our inner self. Through will power we can draw more cosmic energy into our chakras, which will express that life force into our physical system and help maintain our youth and vigor. As we raise ourselves to higher states of consciousness and maintain that higher energy field, we will reduce the amount of conditioned, illusionary consciousness that causes aging. The chronological age of the body has little connection with being young. If you are sixty or seventy years old but take good care of yourself, you can have the biology of a thirty-five-year-old. How well your physiological systems are functioning makes all the difference. To have a happy state of mind does wonders for the body, as opposed to having a weak, anxious mind that ages us prematurely.

I have always loved playing tennis, as it gives me a complete workout for my entire system. I probably inherited my love for tennis from my father, who has a great passion for the sport. I feel as though I am meditating on the court, placing all my attention on that ball, hitting with precision and returning the ball to the other side of the court. When I am playing, no other world exists for me. That's as good a definition of one-pointed mind as I can think of. I am fully energized after playing two sets of singles and never feel the least bit tired or weak. Even as I have grown older, I have felt as if I were carrying the energy field of a twenty-year-old. I always feel tremendous energy that is never depleted no matter how much physical activity I indulge in each day. When we are in control of our mind, anything is possible. I have never paid any attention to my chronological age, as it has never corresponded to my inner strength.

As beneficial as these effects may be in our daily life, the true goal of meditation is to achieve Self-realization, to become conscious of and familiar with our inner being, and to reach the Source, or Oneness, that is the sole purpose of life. Human life is the highest realm in which the possibility exists for the soul to reclaim its identity with the Divine after many incarnations of upward evolution, and meditation is the direct path. All other means discipline the body and prepare us for spiritual advancement, but in my experience only meditation will take us to a higher state of consciousness where we can attain the realization of Truth.

All the great spiritual masters of whom we know are said to have meditated in one way or another. The Buddha achieved his enlightenment during an extended period of meditation and taught the practice as an essential part of his path to liberation from suffering. Although Jesus did not apparently teach meditation per se, the Gospels tell us that he often withdrew from his disciples to be alone in the desert or the mountains, and many reliable sources say that he resided in India and Tibet for some time, to meditate. Muhammad went to a cave on Mount Hera to meditate, and that was where he began to receive revelations. Although meditation is known by different names—sometimes called centering prayer, insight, circulation of inner energy, or repetition of the divine name or names—the essence of the practice is similar in all spiritual traditions.

The greatest contribution to humanity we can make is to learn to leave our normal state of consciousness and move toward our higher Self. Then we can be of help to the world in so many ways. As Amma says, "Purify yourself first, then you can do a lot of work in this world. Self-realize first."

From my own experience, however, I have come to understand that reaching the highest meditative state is not for everyone, because not everyone is ready. It can become at times unrewarding and rigid. It is a hard and lonely road to take all the way through to final liberation, so it's only natural to wonder how to know whether we are ready or not. When we are ready, we receive definite indications, such as losing interest in worldly affairs and other signs that I described in previous chapters. The invitation comes from the Divine when the time is right; there is a strange pull that takes the mind inward while we meditate. It is hard to define what precisely constitutes the right time. Something that can help is to listen to or read the testimony of mystics who have been there before. Here are the words of two such mystics:

- David Hawkins: "It is actually extremely rare for a human to be committed to spiritual truth to the degree of seriously seeking Enlightenment, and those who do make the commitment do so because they are actually destined for Enlightenment."[2]
- Nisargadatta Maharaj: "The impulse always comes from within. Unless your time has come, you will have neither the desire nor the strength to go for Self-Realization wholeheartedly."[3]

I did not begin my meditations out of a desire to learn a specific technique. It really doesn't matter what technique one uses, since all methods get dissolved as meditation deepens, and eventually meditation itself guides us. The unfoldment of my inner growth began on its own, without any anticipation or active pursuit of any goal. Instead, at the right time in life the inherent impulse to meditate spontaneously arose within me in a systematic, progressive manner. My spiritual anguish had become so intense and focused that I wanted nothing more than to end this relative existence and to become liberated in this very life.

Liberation or Immortality

Where there is liberation there are no worldly enjoyments, and where there are worldly enjoyments there is no liberation. But once we experience grace of the Divine, worldly enjoyment and liberation go hand in hand.

SWAMI MUKTANANDA[4]

Life is a struggle, and I did not want to go through this cycle of life and rebirth over and over again in countless lifetimes on earth. (And thank God we can't recall our past life struggles!) We can end this fate, a process called reincarnation, only by becoming Self-realized—meaning that we have recognized our soul for the Divine itself. We continue to stay in this physical body, retaining that higher state, enjoying the cosmic play without becoming troubled by worldly concerns. Once Self-realization takes place and we consciously integrate that into our daily living, we have no need to incarnate again.

The cosmic principle of reincarnation, tied in with the law of cause and effect, or karma, has been embraced by many Hindus, Buddhists, and even early Christian theologians, as well as by philosophers of both East and West. Yogananda was one of the most knowledgeable Indian authors to write about the connections between Eastern and Western religions. He pointed out that, although the Christian Church removed the idea of reincarnation from many of the earliest Christian writings and from Jesus's own teachings, the concept remains in passages from both the Old and New Testaments. As an example, Yogananda quotes the words of Jesus in the book of Revelation (3:11): "Him that overcometh will I make a pillar in the temple of my God, and he shall go no more out". He goes on to comment:

> Here Jesus distinctly refers to the doctrine of reincarnation, saying that when a soul overcomes by spiritual discipline his mortal desires accrued through contact of matter, that soul becomes a pillar of immortality in the everlasting mansion of Cosmic Consciousness;

> and, having found fulfillment of all his desires in Spirit, that soul has no more to be reborn on earth through the karmic reincarnating force of unsatisfied desires.[5]

The most difficult aspect of life consists in living with false perceptions and crushing discontent. We all operate by these conditioned behavioral patterns of which we are almost totally unaware, and yet we should be able to undo this way of life and live to our full potential. We should be able to reach a stage where we can recognize the false as false and true as the true. That is the stage at which we become free and totally liberated by achieving enlightenment.

But what do we mean by liberation? During the earlier years of my spiritual practice I myself used to be confused by this word. Now I see that it does not refer to some state of bondage from which we need to be freed. It is more about freeing ourselves from all the false ideas, attachments, and mental illusions about the past and future that we tend to hang on to at all costs. We accept all these perceptions as if they were our permanent reality, not seeing the falseness of it all. In that sense, liberation, or immortality as some call it, does not mean having a long, perfect life, or many continuous lives, or life after death. It means simply that our mortal consciousness—which we sometimes call the soul, or our individualized spirit—experiences union with the Supreme Consciousness. When we finally feel or experience the presence of the Absolute, we are liberated, free, and immortal (all three words mean the same thing). Meditation prepares the mind to absorb itself into ultimate Universal Consciousness, so we experience liberation. Once we perceive the true reality, it frees our mind from delusion. All the attachments, cravings, and rules that we set for ourselves through our life no longer have any meaning. As a result we experience the great relief of freedom and happiness that is beyond birth and rebirth; that happens naturally through meditation, where the real transformation takes place.

According to Swami Vivekananda, "There is no liberation without the realization that the individual soul and supreme soul are identical in essence, and this liberation, in order to be true must be attained/realized before death."[6] This is a hard concept to understand, as we tend to view life from a limited perspective whereby the mind does not have the capacity to discern truth from falsehood. We are accustomed to believing that our life circumstances will make us happy, if only we can get them right. We are conditioned with a conventional perception that we will be happy only when we get the biggest possible fix of success, money, sex, or status, even if we suspect that it's not worth struggling for achievement, recognition, and power. By creating a world of our own and putting ourselves at the center of it, we throw everything out of focus. We always seem to want more, and we are burdened with false hopes, ideas, beliefs, conditioned behavior patterns, attachments, miseries, and sickness. "Liberation of the soul calls for renunciation of desires," says Vivekananda, "not their multiplication."[7]

All our desires are dualistic in nature because they originate from assuming false identities and continuously defending those identities. We experience a constant struggle between our inner reality and the image we need to present to outside world. We are in a perpetual state of confusion, anxiety, fear, and discontentment, constantly searching for happiness in external places. We are led down a vicious cycle of pleasure and pain, attachment and aversion that ends the same way every time because our senses and intellect are limited. This is why we have to do the deep inner work of Self-realization to liberate ourselves. The spiritual path leads us away from our addiction to the material world by showing us that the eternal state of happiness occurs only when we finally see through the illusion of the manifest world into our deepest sense of Self, the Divine within. Only after realization do we come to know our true nature, seeing beyond the illusory self, and acquire an authentic sense of freedom, letting go of the demands imposed on us by other people. A special harmonization takes place within us and lets us feel that there never can be a chance of error or failure in anything we do. We come to know the driving force within that continuously guides us throughout our existence. With this knowledge comes an unexplainable contentment. Abiding by the cosmic law, we know with certainty that life goes on as it is destined.

I came to realize that living with a false perception of life and repeating everything all over again in another lifetime not only would be difficult, but also was part of a cycle I wanted to end. I could not imagine repeating the same life cycle with all its distress. As I mentioned above, we don't recall our previous births, but if we did we would no doubt discover that in those lives we have gone through similar progressions from birth to adulthood, earning a living and raising a family, then suffering disease, old age, and death. That knowledge of endless life cycles was what prompted the Buddha to seek enlightenment at any cost—to get off the Wheel of Life, as he called it. And so, I felt that I had received an insight from the Divine, that I had the opportunity to pursue realization with full force, to end the cycle and reunite in full consciousness with the Source in this life. We tend to take the fact of our human birth for granted, but the great masters had just the opposite understanding. "Rare is it to be born a human being," the Buddha said, "rarer still to have heard of enlightenment, and even rarer still to pursue it."[8] And the great eighth-century Indian Advaita philosopher Shankaracharya said, "Only through God's grace may we obtain those three rarest advantages—human birth, the longing for liberation, and discipleship to an illumined teacher."[9] The reason they saw life as a rare spiritual opportunity was that, as the Buddha believed, only human beings can achieve enlightenment and step outside the cycle of rebirth. I think we should treasure this opportunity with gratitude.

Nothing is possible without divine intervention, and we will not be able to experience the reality without divine will. How much effort we put in with each meditation and how sincere our devotion and trust are makes a lot of difference in achieving higher states, as does the work we may have done in previous incarnations. I sensed this strongly enough that I was motivated to do whatever it might take to make this my final go-round on what the Buddha called the Wheel of Existence. Once I became proficient in my meditations, they became a fixed part of my routine. In the beginning I was getting up at five a.m. to meditate in the mornings and ending my day with meditation between one and two a.m. One day I was not feeling well and did not have the energy to follow my regular meditation schedule. Yet I was more concerned that I was missing my meditations than that I was unable to fulfill my other obligations. Because I had not yet reached the point at which I could meditate anywhere or in any position, there were days when I was unable to meditate for long hours. Though eventually I would learn that I did not have to be in a sitting posture to meditate, at the time I felt frustrated and prayed that my body would get better soon so that I could get back to daily sitting. I was relieved when, a few days later, I recovered from my illness and was able to resume my proper meditation regimen. Meditation became my passion—the only thing that mattered and the only thing I looked forward to.

Over time, I gave up many activities that I once considered fun. I eliminated most socializing, traveling, watching TV, and many of the things that used to fill my leisure hours. Instead, as my husband once commented, I could be found "either underneath a tree (meditating), at a flat surface with lines (tennis courts), or in a gym." There was no limit to my obsession and preoccupation with keeping my body fit so that it could endure the impact of the deep meditation I was doing. My husband's job, which is his passion, entailed quite a bit of traveling overseas. For years I had accompanied him because I felt it was my wifely duty and because it was a good opportunity to see other parts of the world. But once I became obsessed with meditation, I no longer felt compelled to indulge myself with traveling. I encouraged him to pursue his passion without my company. Even though I did not like being by myself initially, this ceased to bother me as I came to spend most of my day in meditation. Indeed, my husband's busy travel schedule and his appetite for his job gave me the perfect excuse to stay alone at home for weeks at a time and pursue what I was destined to do, with ease. It was as if I were leading a secluded life. This allowed me to extend my meditation time further without any interruptions, so I was able to take it to a higher level.

Over the next couple of years, I continued attending the annual retreat at Amma's ashram in India. I also sought any opportunity to meet with Amma outside the retreat during her travels. As my meditations progressed, myriad of questions arose that needed clarification and that I believed only she could answer. She had gotten to know me well through the years and was aware of the progress I had been making in my meditations. When we were together she could see how my energy moved through each chakra, as well as the increased intensity, as the purification of my body continued. With continuous practice, the one-pointed state in which the mind is completely focused on the object of its attention became steadfast for me, usually occurring the moment I began to meditate. My diligent practice of continuous long hours made it so that the meditations came spontaneously, as though reminding me to meditate even during the daytime while I was engaged with other tasks, calling me in a creative way to close my eyes and just be. Many times I would follow the invitation and sit somewhere, closing my eyes for a few minutes and letting the inner energy flow through me.

I also noted another sign: my ajna, or brow, chakra vibrated intensely and created a kind of pressure around my forehead, to the point where I simply had to meditate. The minute I sat and closed my eyes to meditate, I went into utmost quietude and reached a higher energy field. This happened not only when I meditated, but at other times as well. For example, whenever I indulged in some activity of a spiritual nature, such as listening to devotional songs or discourses or visiting specific temples, or whenever I was in physical proximity to a truly illumined teacher, my awareness automatically shifted to a higher dimension. It felt at times as though someone had turned on a switch within me and all my nerve centers, especially my ajna chakra, began to vibrate continuously. I have read that this can happen to some people when their inner etheric system of chakras is cleared and some or all their higher chakras become activated, bypassing our innate ego resistance. Normally all the nerves of the human body vibrate at a certain frequency, producing internal sounds, unless one has ailments that disrupt these natural vibrations. Otherwise the inner system will respond favorably to certain types of sounds, including religious music and mantras, taking us to a higher vibrational field. One can feel the soothing vibration of that higher energy field, as I have felt many times.

It began to happen that when I was extremely tired from physical activity, instead of sleeping or taking a nap, all I had to do was sit few minutes in my quietude. As a result of continuous practice each day at the same time and place, I reached the samadhi state spontaneously; staying there for a while infused me with an immense amount of energy and peace, the equivalent of a couple of hours of deep sleep. Even today, sitting in quietude has a refreshing effect on my system.

Ongoing Meditation

If you have been able to follow the simple meditation guidelines I described at the end of chapter 2, you will gradually increase the length of time you are able to sit in meditation and feel comfortable. After that, meditation itself will guide you with internal cues, and you will notice a great deal of improvement. You may find, for instance, that you can spontaneously sit for more than the five or ten minutes you originally did. You may also notice that your breathing has deepened and that it has become slower and smoother. As this happens, leave yourself a little more time each day to practice meditation. That doesn't necessarily mean that you'll use up all that time, but more often than not you may continue longer than you expected. But also take care to go easy on yourself. If you miss a day or two, that's not an excuse to throw in the towel altogether. Even five minutes of intensive meditation is better than none at all.

With sincere practice, your clear intention, interest, and yearning to know the Truth will move you forward, and your meditations eventually will become powerful. The more you practice, the deeper the experience will be. Make sure you are clear about the purpose and the goal of your meditation. Is it simply to gain good health and maintain a harmonious daily life, or is it to reach realization of your true nature?

TEN
The Power of Awakened Inner Energy, or Kundalini

Every spiritual tradition describes our inner energy in its own way, but they all see it as the transformative energy that stays dormant within each of us until it is awakened. The Japanese call it ki; the Chinese call it chi; Christians refer to it as Holy Spirit; and in Indian culture it is the kundalini, prana shakti—the supreme spiritual energy that is worshiped as the Divine Mother of the universe or the Cosmic Consciousness. This supreme biolelectrical energy moves and sustains all creation. When awakened in the human body, kundalini unfolds to higher states of consciousness and perception.

In Sanskrit kundalini means "coiled up" and has traditionally been pictured as a serpent coiled at the base of the spine. In its external aspect, kundalini energy is apparent in the limitless functions it performs through the mind and senses, providing the motivating power for all our worldly activities. It controls and maintains our whole physiological system of digestion, circulation, respiration, and muscle movement. In its inner aspect, however, the cosmic reservoir of pranic energy stays hidden until awakened through meditation and other spiritual practices. As Swami Muktananda said, even though kundalini is functioning inside us, we don't perceive her consciously. "Only through subtle understanding can we come to know Her; without understanding, we cannot find Her. This understanding arises when the inner energy becomes active."[1] Then it culminates in conscious samadhi that leads us back to the Source, the Cosmic Consciousness.

Sri Aurobindo has said that "the central motive," the purpose of our life on Earth, is "to awaken, to develop and finally to reveal in a total manifestation the Spirit which is hidden at the center of matter."[2] Given the proper discipline, the awakened kundalini will then guide us to liberate the Spirit. Because we can't comprehend our true nature, or Self, through the normal perception of our senses, we need the awakened inner energy to open a new channel of perception that makes possible intuitive knowledge. When our intellect is purified we are able to see the one indivisible reality that manifests in all forms, the Divinity present in everything. "The effulgent Kundalini, which illuminates the mind, the intellect, the senses and their objects," Muktananda concludes, "also illuminates Herself and makes Herself known."[3]

The transcendental experience of the "emptiness," or "void," that some mystics have written about is possible only after you have awakened the inner energy and it rises to the crown chakra and becomes established there. I should explain that there's a big difference between kundalini that is awakened and kundalini that is active. The most common way for kundalini to become active is through deep meditation. You'll know it's active when your head feels dense and drowsy—at least initially—because a new potent life energy is moving very fast internally. That may sound paradoxical, but until you get used to it, all that energy can feel heavy. There are other ways to activate the inner energy, but in my experience, intensive meditation is the quickest, most effective route to realization.

It does not seem to matter how many rituals we follow, how much yoga we practice, how many mantras we chant, or how many spiritual books we read—we have absolutely no way to realize the Self without the inner energy being awakened. Self-realization will take place when we reach the point where we are ready to awaken as a result of having attained enough inner growth and development, whether in our previous lives or in this life.

I have heard that certain types of drugs and herbs can induce a kundalini awakening, but those methods are not only unreliable, but also potentially dangerous. Even though those methods may temporarily create a shift in the consciousness, the shift will most likely not be lasting and may even create problems down the road. An awakening brought about through meditation is much more gradual and genuine, and the extended state of awareness we perceive as a result is clear and accurate, with no distortion in perception. Once we experience expanded consciousness, it leaves a permanent impact on the mind and instills in us a belief in the existence of a higher power.

When you awaken your inner energy through meditation, the process is easier, more systematic, and more under the control of the meditator. If you have an adverse reaction to a drug or entheogenic substance, such as LSD or peyote, you can't easily turn it off, whereas you can easily come out of a meditative state.

You will also need to integrate the effects of awakening into your everyday life, as I'll explain in more detail shortly. The rate at which this integration takes place depends on the health of the meditator's nervous system and level of psychological development. Yogananda has pointed out that the brain must evolve along with the rest of the nervous system. We have to abide by the principles of cosmic and natural law and remain in good health to be able to withstand the rigors of the awakening process. Along with the need to maintain ethical and physical well-being, as I've noted, we also have to be at the right evolutionary stage, perhaps over many lifetimes. When the time is right, though, the energy can be aroused spontaneously, even in those who have not made much spiritual preparation or who have been practicing meditation for just a short time. This is probably due to the fact that their evolutionary preparedness has brought them to that point. Once the brain and nervous system have reached the right state of maturity, they need only a slight or moderate effort to lead to a higher state.

Most of us are unaware of this dormant energy unless and until it is somehow awakened. The energy resides in the root chakra, the first of the seven subtle energy centers, and when activated it uncoils and starts to rise up the spine, through the central nerve channel, until it unites with pure consciousness above the crown of the head. Books have been written about the chakras themselves, so without getting into too much detail, let me explain as best I can how they function within us.

The word *chakra* comes from a Sanskrit root meaning "wheel," and these energy centers have been likened by some to the wheels of a chariot—the most powerful vehicle in ancient India at the time when the system was first identified. Each chakra is a concentrated center that resembles a hub from which life-giving energy radiates to the rest of the body. Like transformers, they absorb the pranic energy from the universe that is always around us and convert it into frequencies that our energy system needs to function. Interpenetrating our physical body, the chakras have a close relationship with our glandular functions. Their basic health affects our physical health and functionality on a daily basis. Unhealthful diet and behaviors, including misuse of prescription drugs and other stimulants such as alcohol and tobacco, can damage these chakras and render them inflexible. This reduces our vital energy distribution to the whole system, obstructs our spiritual progress, and makes us prone to various health problems caused by glandular dysfunction. When the chakras are healthy and fully functioning, they intensify our awareness and we can feel their vibration during meditation.

The chakras lie along the sushumna, or central nerve channel, and interconnect with two other important channels on either side of the sushumna, called the *ida* and the *pingala*. The ida and pingala originate at the base of the spine and go upward spirally, alternating from left to right and from right to left, forming a loop around each chakra. Through these seven centers, divine primordial energy descends into the body from the crown chakra at the top of the head and is stored in a place called the *hara*, corresponding to the abdomen or belly, about four inches below the navel.

Although the chakras overlap somewhat, each one corresponds to a specific area of the body and is associated with certain nerve ganglia in that vicinity. The first, or root, chakra (Sanskrit name, *muladhara*) corresponds to the perineum at the base of the spine, where the body comes in contact with the earth when seated in meditation. It is associated with the adrenal glands and the legs, the element earth, and the sense of smell. It provides support and balance to the body and our basic physiological needs. We also associate the root chakra with survival, especially through the extended family, clan, or tribe.

The second chakra (*svadisthana*) corresponds to the lumbar and sacral regions and the genitals and is associated with the reproductive organs, urogenital system, bladder, and kidneys. The element associated with this chakra is water, symbolic of pleasure and self-gratification. This chakra governs the sense of taste, our sexuality (and, by extension, money and power), and vital prana.

The third chakra (*manipura*) corresponds to the solar plexus, located between the navel and the tip of the breastbone. It is associated with the pancreas, liver, and digestive system, the element of fire, and the sense of sight. On a psychological level, this chakra governs our self-esteem.

Taken together, the first three are often called the lower chakras, not so much because of their location but because they regulate the impulses of survival and self-importance. But it would be a mistake to minimize their significance. Just as you cannot build a tall edifice without a strong foundation, so you cannot develop a fully integrated personality without strong lower chakras that ground you to the earth and everyday life. Some spiritual practitioners who have focused foremost on developing the higher chakras have acknowledged running into problems when they had to confront issues of family, sex, money, and self-esteem.

The bridge between the lower and higher energy centers is the fourth, or heart, chakra (*anahata*), which corresponds to the heart, lungs, circulation, and the thymus (a gland that is located between the heart and the breastbone and is part of the immune system). The heart chakra is associated with love and emotions in general, the sense of touch, and the element of air. Opening the heart center is believed by many to be the first step in spiritual maturity, developing compassion for others as a bridge to ultimate union with Divine Love.

Located at the base of the neck, the fifth chakra (*vishuddha*) is associated with the throat, thyroid gland, ears, and mouth. Its element is the ether, or *akasha*, a Sanskrit term defined as the first material element created from the astral world. This chakra governs the principle of sound, in the sense of communication—both by hearing others and through self-expression. By extension, then, it is the center of will, as we make decisions and express choices by "speaking our truth."

The *third eye* is the traditional term for the sixth chakra (ajna), corresponding to the space between the eyebrows. This chakra is the command center and is associated with the cognitive faculties of the mind, including reason and intuition, as well as the left eye, the nose, spine, ears, and pineal gland. It is all about perception, both inner and outer vision, including vision of the future.

The seventh, crown chakra (*sahasrara*), the seat of higher awareness, corresponds to the top of the cranium and the uppermost part of the cerebrum and is associated with the right eye and the pituitary gland. Its Sanskrit name means "thousand-petaled," referring to the fountains of light that are said to stream from this chakra at the moment of enlightenment. This is the final meeting place, where the individualized soul unites with the Supreme Universal Consciousness and pranic energy reaches its highest point. Immortality is achieved when we reach this chakra and the illusion of individual self is dissolved.

Normally these chakras are blocked by the karmic accumulations from countless births. Once the inner energy starts its activation, it removes the karmic blockages of each chakra in succession, by sending increased amounts of pranic life energy through the channels of the subtle body. During meditation you can feel the intense vibration of each chakra if they have been purified completely.

I learned from Amma that there are three *granthis*, or knots, representing three levels of psychophysical life, which are located in different regions of the body and which cause most of our ailments by serving as barriers to the free flow of prana. The first and second chakras together form the first knot, called the *Brahma granthi*. The third and fourth chakras form the second knot, the *Vishnu granthi*; and the fifth and sixth chakras form the third knot, or *Rudra granthi*. All health problems are caused by the accumulation of karma from many prior births, which closes these knots so that the inner energy can't climb up and reconnect us to the Divine.

According to Amma, the first knot is connected with issues of the nervous system and the capacity of red blood cells to carry oxygen. The second knot relates to problems with the digestive and circulatory systems. And the third knot can block cell rejuvenation and the proper balance of prana. When prana flow is restricted to the region of the first knot, instinctive drives, including hunger and sensual pleasure, dominate the system. The second knot involves our emotional life, and the third, our intellect. When desires and impulses originating in the lower chakras become strong, the flow of prana gets stuck at the first knot and very little pranic energy reaches the higher chakras.

As inner energy is activated by intensive meditation, it has the ability to break through these three knots in succession. But the piercing of any chakra can result in extreme discomfort and uneasiness as the system is adjusted to maintain the demands of this new energy. The whole body has to adapt to the new pattern of consciousness, because the entire system is undergoing a change. Once the purification is finished, the energy finally moves upward to the seventh chakra and reaches its destination. As Muktananda says, only when the third knot is opened can we experience true samadhi. At this point the body is completely purified. If each chakra is not purified, or if all the blockages are not removed from our previous karmic actions in sequence, the great serpent energy cannot climb to the crown of the head and explode in geysers of light.

Along with intense meditation and devotion to God, the merit accumulated from spiritual practices performed in a person's past births can also cause inner energy to be awakened. There is one more way, which I mentioned in chapter 6, which is through shaktipat, a direct physical contact by a highly illumined teacher, provided the individual is receptive and open. Even then, however, the seeker must work hard for the awakened energy to ascend, because activation of the energy alone does not bring realization.

And so, even after I knew that my inner energy had been awakened, I was still aware that it would not start ascending toward the highest state without continued effort.

I was already spending several hours a day in meditation, yet this practice did not seem to be enough to achieve my goal of reaching higher states of consciousness. Even with all my household activities, I still needed to meditate longer hours without any other concerns. I was determined to give up just about anything to raise my energy, but to my surprise it was not as easy as I had imagined.

As a result of extending the amount of time I spent in deep meditation, the energy did finally start its upward movement, piercing each chakra in succession. This process is hard to control, and that's why it was so important to maintain strict discipline in eating, exercise, and rest and, most of all, by never missing meditation sessions. Though I had been meditating for some years, I noticed many changes after I returned from my two-week intense meditation retreat with Amma. Meditations were effortless, and I felt a kind of spontaneous ease that was different from anything I had experienced before. I felt as if *real* meditation began only after your inner energy had been activated—as if the inner energy had now been given permission to start working toward its goal with full force. As the system is illuminated with the awakened energy, the process itself is guided with ease.

I was astonished to sense that this mysterious energy seemed to know its natural pace and to follow the process depending on one's constitution. It understood how much my system could tolerate, and so everything was being controlled by *it* instead of by me. At this stage my desire for meditation only increased, and I often felt uncomfortable and even disoriented if I didn't meditate at least for half an hour.

That was when I remembered that I had received shaktipat from Karunamayi during the three retreats I had attended at her ashram. Although I hadn't felt anything special while she touched me on the forehead or crown, I had sensed a palpable change in my meditations after I returned home. I no longer seemed to have to make a conscious effort to get to a one-pointed state of awareness. I felt a special clarity that I had not experienced before. Through my inner perception, at times I could actually see the upward movement of energy as it appeared to take form in various shapes and colors. I was even able to feel the vibration of each chakra as the inner energy was working through it. My mind no longer consciously controlled how things appeared in this new field of consciousness, and I felt as though it had been waiting for some force to give it a push to get started—and Amma's shaktipat had provided the needed impetus.

Once I had been awakened like this, there was no going back. The evolution of consciousness had started, and finally I knew I would be going home. I felt utter confidence that the realization of my True Self would take place, that it would reveal itself as pure Being and infinite freedom.

"Liberation while still living is considered to be the highest experience," Ajit MookerJee, an acknowledged expert on the sacred texts of India, remarks. "It is the fusion of the individual energy with the universal energy, and the cosmic power reveals itself through the body."[4]

From all the difficulties I experienced during the process, however, I understood that once the energy is active it does not just shoot up in a straight line to reach its goal of opening the crown chakra. There is a definite process and a system to its progression. Each stage of its unfolding unties the knots of different energies, and this clearing brings transformation at every stage. As noted, it also resulted in extreme discomfort in various parts of my body as the energy started moving and pierced each chakra. I had heard that the initial movements through the first three chakras are the most difficult, because the knots and karmic blockages are heavier there. How long it takes this energy to purify each chakra varies with every person and his or her karmic load. Some take many years and others finish in a short time. In my case, once the energy started climbing upward, purification took almost two years before I experienced my illuminated Self.

ELEVEN
Challenges and Impediments to the Upward Movement of Kundalini

As the kundalini passes through each sensitive subtle nerve center, untying or piercing each knot, we can expect to experience quite a few hurdles on the way. The metamorphosis that one goes through as a result of the awakened kundalini has tremendous impact on the physical body and the nervous system. However, the effects of kundalini awakening cannot be fully explained until one actually experiences it. And so in this chapter, I will describe in detail the challenges I faced as the energy started ascending, and how I coped with each of them in turn.

As the awakened energy reached each chakra, certain physiological functions of my body underwent a progressive transformation. I suffered from digestive issues, backaches, memory problems, insomnia, and extremes of heat. Because I had learned about this process from my reading and other sources, I was somewhat prepared for what lay ahead.

I knew that my nervous system would not be able to handle all the stress on its own, so I adjusted my meditations accordingly. Most of the time I could control the energy at will and was able to move it toward the location of the heart chakra; for whatever reason, the heart chakra can more readily absorb these high levels of energy. As I've mentioned often, the Self does not reveal itself in weak or sick flesh, and I was meticulous about maintaining proper diet, exercise, and rest.

Gopi Krishna, who has written as authoritatively as anyone about the kundalini experience, put the relative danger of kundalini in perspective. "Under the action of a stronger current than that for which it was designed," he writes, "any man-made mechanism, even a hundredth part as sensitive and intricate as the human frame, would be wrecked or damaged immediately."[1] He points out that as the result of evolution, the human body has developed "certain inherent qualities" and "safety devices" that protect us against the release of this potent energy, provided we are in good health and our internal organs are sound.

As the energy ascended to my higher chakras, I went through any number of "partial" realizations, or samadhi states—fleeting experiences of bliss or insight. Each time, I felt as though I had reached the highest state of samadhi, not realizing that there was much further to go. We pass through many stages or gradations of consciousness on the journey of realization. It's often hard to distinguish these intermediate layers, because at the time they feel as if they are our final destination. Each new stage feels so ultimate that it's easy to become confused; that's one reason I have tried to set out in this book a reliable way of recognizing when we have reached the final state of union with the Absolute. The degree of transformation that each of us experiences varies according to our capacity and evolutionary progress. We experience the pure radiance that shines as our True Self only when the final realization takes place. Our false, egoic self falls away and our True Self takes over and runs the show. Ultimately, the mind is capable of distinguishing clearly what is real and what is not.

I noticed a change in my meditations as I began to feel uncomfortable and uneasy the minute I closed my eyes. I felt unusual sensations within various areas of my body, including a strange throbbing vibration all over my head. My ajna chakra started to vibrate heavily and continuously, to a point that I thought my head was going to split in half from the pressure. My heart started beating rapidly, and beads of sweat formed on my forehead from the increased heat, making me wonder if I might be having a heart attack. I became so restless and uneasy that I could not continue meditating, but had to open my eyes, get up, and walk around for some time before I tried again. Even after a break, I was hesitant to go back to meditating, for fear of facing such overwhelming energy. The situation had become unbearable at times.

I had been accustomed to sensations of calm and peace when meditating, so this new experience was doubly unsettling. I had expected the peace to grow deeper, but I realized that a deeper level of peace comes only after attaining the final point of enlightenment, when the inner energy reaches our top chakra. As much as I had read and heard about the power of inner energy, I was still caught off guard. In the years I had been meditating, I had never once felt so much heat emanating from within myself. This condition would last for the first half hour or so, depending on how much I could withstand, and then it would calm down and I would feel better. Gradually I was able to tolerate the inner heat and turmoil a bit longer, and as I did so I became more acclimated to the change. Like anything else, resisting the new situation only made it worse.

What concerned me most, however, was that these sudden changes to my system were limiting the length of time I could meditate. My heart was pumping so profoundly, for instance, that I started to check my blood pressure, as I had learned to do, with a simple device. To my alarm both the systolic and diastolic readings were unusually high. When this persisted for several days, I forced myself to see a doctor, even though I knew deep down that my elevated blood pressure could be due to the new energy. My doctor suggested that I take medication to bring the pressure down, but I refused and told him I would control it with proper diet and exercise. I wanted to avoid taking medication, as I was fully aware of the reason for my hypertension, but I had no desire to explain this to the doctor. In the end I continued to meditate, with the hope that my body would eventually accommodate itself to the changes and my blood pressure would normalize.

Soon after, I began to notice a tingling sensation, as if something were crawling on my back, neck, and other parts of my body. The itching sensation this created, especially around my neck region, made it extremely taxing, although it disappeared completely after several weeks. In addition to the continual throbbing pain around my forehead, my eyes often became stressed and red after meditation. I had read that this could happen because the chakras around the optic nerve were being activated, so I was not alarmed. I simply used eyedrops so that no one would notice the redness.

There was an increased amount of saliva in my mouth while I was meditating. I had to get up to spit it out, as it made me uncomfortable. That wasn't so bad, but later another issue arose with my throat: every night for over a month it became so parched that I had to get up constantly and moisten it with water. I learned to keep a water bottle next to my bed at night, although thirst was not the cause of this odd sensation. It was as though a subtle current of energy were passing through a straight, tube-like channel, leaving it dry as dust.

My sleep was further interrupted by another disturbing occurrence. I started to develop heart palpitations. This continued for some time, but I grew accustomed to them and was able to ignore them completely.

The net result of all these physical disturbances was that trying to meditate became a huge task compared to the joy it had been before. I became apprehensive of what might happen each day as a result of my meditation. But this did not stop me, and I kept on, confident in the knowledge that all these things would eventually subside. Sometimes I felt as if such a high voltage of electricity were passing through my body that I might die or break apart. There seemed to be some kind of life-and-death struggle taking place within me, over which I had no control. I learned to relax as much as possible despite all these issues and tried to focus more on concentration.

For a long time, nights were intolerable. The minute I closed my eyes to sleep I felt extreme heat or sensations of electricity. At first I didn't understand why this happened mainly at night. It seemed that for the inner energy to perform its purification work, the body needed to be motionless. I did occasionally feel the heat coming and going during the day, but that didn't bother me, because I was busy carrying out my daily tasks. But on some nights there was so much heat and vibration that I had to get out of bed and either sit down or walk around, without disturbing anyone, until it passed. This happened at least four or five times every night, for five to eight minutes at a time. For several months, sleep was a rare commodity, as this energy was surging through my whole body constantly. My whole system had been thrown off its normal rhythm and my body was in complete disorder. I had forgotten how it feels to have a good night's sleep without having to wake up every hour or two.

I was used to going to sleep at one or two a.m., by which time my husband was already asleep in bed and all I could see was a night light or some moonlight coming in through the windows. But one night as I entered my bedroom, I could see no light at all, even with my eyes wide open. I had undergone a sudden shift in my consciousness and felt as if I was in the middle of what I can only call a nothingness or emptiness. This formlessness seemed to be made up of all consciousness, without any boundaries or material obstructions. I could not see where I was going or where my bed was, and had to grope in the utter darkness to find my bed. When I closed my eyes, I saw the same formless consciousness. Although I was aware of my body, I felt I had nothing and I was simply moving at that particular moment. Everything was just empty space—space and more space. I would blink my eyes a couple of times, hoping to snap out of it, but this state would still last several minutes before I slowly shifted back to my normal consciousness.

One of the first troubling occurrences was a pain in my left lower back, along my hip. I was unable to sit, lie down, or move around without pain, for a long time. This throbbing sensation persisted for quite a few weeks, and when the pain reached a heightened level I sought out medical advice. X-rays did not show any abnormality or other reason for the discomfort. I eventually went to physical therapy a couple of times, as I was unable to bend without constant pain. Once again, though, the pain moderated only when it was ready, it seemed. I also experienced high-pitched ringing sounds at times of the day, and all I could do was wait for them to pass.

As the energy continued moving upwards, I started feeling depressed much of the time, along with a kind of boredom after every meditation. Returning to my normal consciousness and attending to my accustomed activities no longer felt satisfying, as if I was just going through the motions. And yet when I went on retreats, attended various conferences or talks that other teachers gave on spiritual philosophy, or found myself in the company of other seekers, I was quite active and happy.

I found it especially disturbing when I became grouchy and impatient toward everyone, annoyed with everything I needed to do after coming back from meditation. Going "back to normal" required a big effort on my part, and I usually preferred being by myself. That was difficult, since I had to fulfill all the responsibilities of a wife and mother and take care of so many household tasks. Some days I felt loneliness so intense that I experienced long episodes of crying, feeling as if I did not belong here any longer and did not know *where* I belonged. I felt very aloof toward the outside world and everyone around me. The gap seemed to have widened more between the outer and inner world. I felt more connected and contented being within myself. As I continued to function on autopilot, I made sure to keep all worries and concerns to myself, waiting patiently to talk with my teacher during my visits with her.

In addition to the three annual retreats I attended with Amma in India, I also visited her when she came to America during her tours. I was grateful for her support and guidance and was able to discuss any and all my problems without hesitation. But when I was away from her, I missed her so much and wished she were always next to me, because she was everything for me.

Though I would have liked to talk to Amma about all the issues that arose, unless they were intolerable and persistent I pretty much handled them on my own. When I began having stiffness and cramping in my neck and shoulder areas, for instance, I became uneasy and nervous, wondering what now? The trouble might have been caused by the energy being moved toward my throat chakra, but I wasn't certain. So I tried various yogic exercises and stretches each day, for at least an hour, in an attempt to ease the pain, and that helped at times. But regardless of what I tried to do to eliminate this and other pains and discomforts, they never completely dissipated until the purification of my chakras was finished.

The coming and going of pain and discomfort was unpredictable. For a time I struggled with constant heat and an intense vibration in my hands and feet during the day. As a result of this, my hands and feet always looked flushed, and at times my whole body felt like it was on fire—as if a surplus amount of pranic energy was concentrated in certain areas of my body, especially in my hands. I had a strong intuitive sense that this inner energy that emanated through my hands could heal anything automatically, could cure all the injured cells or easily revitalize the weak areas of an entire bodily system. After realizing that this heat and vibration represented the cosmic energy passing through my hands, I decided to take advantage of it. I placed my hands on certain parts of my body where I felt occasional morning arthritic pain or stiffness, and the pain or stiffness would miraculously disappear after few seconds. I knew then that this was the prana shakti that is capable of healing anything instantly. Occasionally I passed this energy to my husband and my children for their well-being, without their knowledge. I felt good that something constructive could come of my suffering. There were days when all my joints were continuously aching; this aching was accompanied by a feverish feeling that I knew was not from the normal environment. Though I felt horrible I got accustomed to ignoring these discomforts, as I was fully aware of the cause.

Of all the problems I encountered, however, the worst were the disturbances in my digestive system, during which it became completely altered. I started getting an unusual pain in my abdomen, accompanied by bloating. Although I knew this was related to the kundalini energy, the fact that I was suffering led me to take action. The discomforts continued for weeks and started getting worse as my excretory function became erratic. Since my eating habits were always impeccable, I knew this disturbance could not have been related to my food intake. Now even a small amount of food was not getting digested properly. I became afraid to eat anything because of what might happen.

With all these worries, I started paying even more attention to my meals and ate with extreme caution. My food had to be easily digestible, nutritious, pure, and of the highest quality, with not too much or too little intake. Any deviation from the balance of moderate intake created so many problems that I regretted having made the mistake of eating more or less than I should have. Since I was never hungry, I did not really want to eat, yet I ate; and although I was not thirsty, I always drank plenty of water.

I could usually figure out exactly which chakra the energy was working on. During my visits with my teacher, she confirmed my knowing, as she could easily tell which of the three granthis was being opened up. She told me to be patient until the purification was finished and to continue with my deep meditations, as the process would be completed soon. She also advised me to drink extra water to help counteract the extreme heat being generated from within. With confidence in her assurances, I was able to keep going with determination, eagerness, and courage.

I've mentioned that I had frequent crying episodes during meditation, and now that started happening again. I burst into tears for no specific reason. This was especially odd for me since I never cried, believing that crying is a sign of losing control of our emotions. But during these crying jags, I was definitely not in control! Instead of grief, however, these episodes were accompanied by feelings of deep, unconditional love. It was as if someone very close to me had just given me a hug, and yet the feeling was unlike any hug I had received from the closest of family members or friends. I recognized it as something no one except your own True Self can give you. It emanated from a new dimension and touched the subtlest region of my heart, a feeling that can't be described in words. All I can say is that when I reached this dimension of feelings and sensations, I knew that the energy had arrived in my heart region—and that the purification would soon continue to move toward my upper chakras. I felt a soothing vibration close to the heart chakra, confirming that it was being worked on. The feeling was so special that I never again experienced anything like it throughout the entire process.

After some time my meditations shifted to another level, and I felt an extreme quietness and focused concentration settle into my entire system. I felt that I could command my inner energy to do anything I wanted. For example, if I wanted to shift my attention from one energy center to another, all I had to do was focus on that particular chakra. I could sit and close my eyes for meditation, and right away my mind went to where it should be. I no longer had to try to concentrate to center my focus as I had in the past. Absolutely no effort was necessary, as everything was being governed by the inner energy.

As I proceeded on the path of purification, with its attendant pains and hazards, the intensity of my longing increased to the point where I wanted to get to my destination and be done with it as soon as I could. At the same time, my faith seemed to increase as I neared the end of the tunnel, and that helped me endure the pain and discomfort of the process.

As the Mother writes, "Spiritual consciousness gives you the deep inner realization, contact with the Divine, liberation from external fetters; but for this liberation to be effective, for it to have an action on the rest of the being, the mind must be open enough to be able to hold the spiritual light of knowledge."[2] In short, your body must be healthy, strong, and disciplined enough and your mind mentally stable enough to withstand the rigors of the process.

As usual I kept everything to myself, knowing that no one would believe my story, as these experiences are extremely rare and I was not prepared to give an elaborate explanation. After some months, I realized that whatever happened did not matter any longer. I was even prepared to die if that was meant to be. I started talking to myself before each meditation, asking my inner self to get me to my final destination without more discomfort to make these episodes less painful and more tolerable. I had nothing to lose at that point.

I felt as if I were living two different lives by hiding all these symptoms from my family and everyone else. But since I could not turn back on the road down which I had started, I believed I had no choice but to manage these challenges on my own.

Finally, all the purification ended and my meditations returned to normal—a smooth ride of immense peace and quiet, as if that huge storm had subsided completely.

Despite that renewed sense of peace and calm, however, I was never my old familiar self again. I even forgot how I used to be before all these changes began. Although I looked very much the same, I had somehow been transformed into a different being.

Insight of an Awakened Inner Energy

The experience of awakened kundalini varies greatly from one individual to another in both its positive and negative aspects and the way it affects the person's perception. This inner energy exists in all of us in its latent form; it is not the exclusive property of only a few, but becomes apparent only after it has been awakened. This awakening can happen as the result of disciplined training and working with an enlightened teacher, but it sometimes arises spontaneously, most often in people doing spiritual work on their own. This may be disorienting if the practitioner isn't aware of what's happening, so it's helpful to know the signs of an inner-energy awakening.

There are many reasons and ways in which one's inner energy is awakened, including one's level of faith, devotion, desire, and intensive meditation. Whether and when the awakening happens may depend on our karmic propensity as well, created by actions and tendencies from past lifetimes or earlier in this life. Eastern and Western cultures use differing terminology to describe it but are talking about essentially the same thing. In the West we are less familiar with the kundalini experience, and doctors and psychologists may have misdiagnosed some people who have gone through some seemingly psychosomatic problems without knowing what was really happening. These medical personnel, not realizing that inner-energy awakening plays a dynamic role in human evolution, taking us through many subtle levels of inner awareness to a direct experience of the oneness of all life, perceive the awakening as a psychological malfunction that requires medical treatment.[3]

In this chapter we have already seen many of the unmistakable signs of an awakening of the kundalini, or inner energy. Keep them in mind in the event they should occur as a result of your ongoing meditation practice.

TWELVE

Deeper States of Meditation and Realization of Self

The kundalini having risen to my crown chakra, I began to feel more at ease with my condition. Although this breakthrough released still more heat into my system, at least the pain and discomfort that my body had endured finally relented. My health and vitality normalized and my stamina gradually increased, so that I felt more invigorated. All the knots of the *vasanas*, or karmic load, became loosened and my past karmas were removed, allowing me to experience the light of the Self without effort.

As I reached this point, I suddenly felt a heightened illumination, a boundless radiance in which the whole field of my consciousness during meditation appeared as a brightly shining sun. This stunning illumination of consciousness was the individualized soul emanating as profound love and was accompanied by an unusual depth of calmness and peace. The soul knows that it is there by its illumination. I was absorbed in this pool of brightness everywhere. The first time I experienced this illumination, which is felt only in the deepest meditative samadhi state, my eyes were filled with tears that slowly rolled down my cheeks.

Being in that dimension, I felt profound gratitude for the experience as it touched my deepest inner core. Finally I was seeing my True Self without any question that this is who we all are—the Divine within human form. There is a definite internal knowing at this point, when we clearly see false as false and true as true. This sense of knowing is so powerful that no confirmation is needed. This realization of the soul gradually transforms into faith by virtue of a strong intuitive knowledge.

Intuition

Normally we relate to the world through our five physical senses. But we also have a sixth sense, the power of intuition that guides us to choose correctly in any given situation. We are all born with this sixth sense, but it generally remains underdeveloped from lack of use. One way to develop the sixth sense is through meditating or spending time in some form of quietude, because that intuitive faculty comes from our inner being, or soul, which is strengthened by meditation. As intuition develops from prolonged meditation, our discriminative insight opens up and can be applied in making decisions of any kind. It is the expression of direct knowledge or vision that bypasses reasoning and deduction. After I had been meditating for years, it seemed that every time I made a decision, it was the correct one, and everything worked out perfectly.

As my intuition developed, I seemed better able to recognize and distinguish character traits in people as soon as I met them. For example, I could simply look at a person or hear that person say a few words and immediately note whether he or she was genuine or pretentious.

Occasionally when I was in a deep meditative state, in utter silence and stillness, I had the sensation of a light suddenly falling like a drop from above. The sensation lasted for just a split second, and at first I did not understand where it was coming from. The impression I had was of something coming from outside or above and penetrating deep into my being, or as if my mind had tapped into a higher mental faculty just for a moment. Even today I can't say exactly where that drop of light came from: the origin was a mystery. It did not come from my brain, because I was fully conscious in the existing field and yet absolutely no thought process was taking place. I knew it was separate and independent of everything else that was happening, so I called it intuitive light.

By now I was in control of the inner energy movement within my body, able to move the energy toward any chakra at any time. I would bring the energy all the way down to the bottom chakra and bring it up again. Once it reached the higher chakras, the pressure became so heavy that I would move the energy from the seventh chakra to the fourth, which reduced the pressure in the forehead and crown region. I did this automatically, without having any prior understanding that, as I have since learned, for the samadhi state to become permanent and well established, one should bring the energy to the heart chakra, which is the final center and ultimate goal of all practice. According to Ramana Maharshi, once the kundalini energy reaches the crown chakra, it should go to the heart chakra, "through what is called the *jivanadi,* which is only a continuation of the sushumna. The sushumna is thus a curve. It apparently starts from the lowest chakra, and rises through the spinal cord to the brain and from there it bends down and ends in the heart."[1]

At this point some thoughts still come and the senses are somewhat active, but the mind shows absolutely no recognition of them and merely ignores them. By now, the question of thoughts seemed unimportant to me. The absence of thoughts is not a prerequisite to obtaining Self-realization, nor does it matter if the mind is active, as long as we are completely embedded in the new dimension of the Self. You hold on to the Self even in the presence of some mental activity. Until reaching this stage, I had never experienced real peace nor known what being happy or contented really meant!

The contentment I'm talking about is quite different from what we feel from acquiring material possessions. The more I experienced the illumination I've just described, the more contented and peaceful I felt with my meditations. And yet at this stage I still seemed to be aware of a state of duality. The radiance of the consciousness I felt at this point was like a reflection on a surface that was much deeper. In retrospect, I now see that there is a difference between this localized illumined consciousness and the pure awareness of emptiness that I later experienced. That advanced stage is a nondualistic state of being in which there is neither subject (meditator) nor object (Divine). There is simply nothingness, the unmanifest state of primordial nature. It is like returning to the uncorrupted consciousness of childhood. Until children develop self-consciousness (the ego of I-me-mine) at a certain age, they carry the beautiful primordial consciousness with which they were born, radiating love for everything and everyone. They emit a high amount of pure energy and their consciousness is not yet fully immersed in the materialistic world. Although they can be selfish at times, they somehow find it easier to express unconditional love than do most grownups. Perhaps this is the reason we always feel relaxed and happy when we are near children.

This reminds me of an incident that happened to me one day while I was walking on a crowded Manhattan street. I paused for a moment to take my cell phone from my purse and as I did, suddenly a small girl, no more than a toddler, ran toward me and held me so tightly that she stopped me from moving any farther. I was startled and glanced down to see who was hugging me with such affection, looking up at my face and smiling. Strange as it may sound, for that moment I did not care who the child belonged to and didn't look around to see where she had come from. All I cared about was giving her the biggest hug I could, touching her face gently with mine just for that moment. Neither of us seemed to care whether any acquaintanceship or family relationship existed between us. I felt a unique love and affection for this child, as though I had known her for some time. And yet I didn't recognize her face and had no recollection of ever having met her before. Finally, I looked around and noticed her mother standing nearby, watching it all with a smile as her child clung to an apparent stranger in the street. I did not hear her calling her toddler back until our encounter was over, and even then she showed no alarm or concern.

This spontaneous expression of love touched my heart because it made me realize how fortunate children are in retaining more of that pure energy than do many of us adults. I thought that this toddler might be recapturing memory from her previous births, in which I might have been part of her life. She may have recognized me—and vice versa, as I felt the same sense of familiarity with her. One of the Christian Gospels tells the story of little children being brought to Jesus for his blessing, only to be turned away by his disciples, who apparently thought the great teacher had better things to do. But Jesus stopped them and said, "Let the little children come to me, and do not hinder them, for the kingdom of heaven belongs to such as these" (Matthew, 19:14. All Bible texts come from the New International Version).

I believe "the kingdom of heaven" was his term for realization, and that to be Self-realized is like returning to the Primordial Consciousness that we are born with. Likewise, my encounter with the spontaneous love of that little child in the street reminded me how soon we lose that pure state. It gets covered over by layers of materialized awareness in its densest form, driven by the ego as we slowly disconnect from the Supreme Consciousness. Until we Self-realize, we all live in the world of dualism. The only times we experience pure Primordial Consciousness are during childhood, before we develop the sense of ego or self, and again after we reclaim the Truth through enlightenment.

That primordial, formless state of awareness is what we ultimately are, the radiance of Self that appears clearly and vividly as our individualized soul. At this stage it has not merged back with the Source of the Self, because we have not yet experienced the ultimate God-realization. That happens only when we reach further into the fourth dimension of pure awareness, in which we abide in oneness in absolute stillness. There can be no consciousness without awareness, but there can be awareness without consciousness, as when we are in our deep-sleep state. We are the awareness of Self when we are sleeping, but we are not conscious of it. However, the bliss we enjoy *consciously* is the fourth state, called Turiya—the bliss of being with our Ultimate Source.

We experience consciousness (True Self) in three distinct states: waking, dreaming, and deep sleep. And of course the fourth state, Turiya, which I will discuss in the next chapter. Three corresponding bodies, called sheaths, encase the soul: the causal body, the astral body, and the physical body. In Vedanta these bodies are known as *kosas*. When we transcend these layers we realize the pure Self. The gross, or physical, body is the outermost layer of high density and has a slow vibrational frequency. Here our consciousness is barely activated with regard to its highest evolutionary potential. At this level Self identifies with the gross body and manifests itself as the ordinary waking consciousness of ego-driven, material existence controlled by the senses and desires and with a limited perception.

The next level, the subtle, or astral, body, is the layer of vitality in which prana animates all the activities of our physical existence. From this subtle level of manifestation we get the ability to analyze all sense data with our intellect. We experience this realm in our normal dream state, where the mind does not express itself through our senses. Our Self identifies with the subtle body and manifests as the dreamer.

Our innermost layer is the causal body, our higher transconceptual mind, where wisdom manifests. In this dimension are stored all our previous accumulated tendencies. When we reach this realm we acquire the ability to awaken the inner energy as all the energy centers and channels are activated and a definite shift in consciousness takes place. This is when our consciousness manifests itself as the deep sleeper. We experience the bliss and undisturbed peace of the True Self but remain completely unaware.

Over many lifetimes our individualized divinity frees itself from all past tendencies and desires connected with the gross, subtle, and causal bodies. We must transcend all three bodies before the Self identifies as individualized pure consciousness. The Self is the main fuel that operates through these three bodies. Without realization of this truth we try to gain happiness from the illusionary world by clutching the three bodies but mostly remaining in the gross body. Only when the Self reclaims its lost divinity and we recognize the radiance of the soul as our inner Divinity do we find utmost peace while in deep meditation. After experiencing this peace, I looked forward to seeing the radiance of the Self every time I meditated. I had an irresistible desire to meditate simply so that I could be with the radiance, because the exuberant light of the Self that appears then is astonishing. I would patiently wait until I was fully absorbed in the radiance before I returned to my normal state. As Yogananda's guru Sri Yukteswar said, "Spiritual advancement is not measured by one's display of outward powers or outward transformation, but solely by the depth of his bliss or peace in meditation."[2]

A famous master of Zen (in China, Ch'an) Buddhism describes Self-realization as "silent Illumination" and goes on to say:

Silently and serenely one forgets all words;
Clearly and vividly it appears before one,
When one realizes it, time is vast and without limit. . . .
In its Essence, it is pure awareness.
Singularly reflecting in this bright awareness,
Full of wonder in this pure reflection . . .
Infinite wonder permeates this serenity;
In this Illumination all intentional efforts vanish.
Silence is the final word.
Reflection is the response to all (manifestation).
Devoid of any effort,
This response is natural and spontaneous . . .
The Truth of silent illumination
Is perfect and complete.

Extensive Records of Ch'an Master Hung-chih Cheng-chueh

At this stage, all desires, grasping, and fear diminished significantly for me. As a result I developed a sense of confidence, along with enhanced powers of discrimination to make the right decisions. It felt like a big weight had been removed, and I felt much lighter and simpler, with utmost satisfaction. At last I could breathe freely, as if the whole atmosphere had changed and I had undergone a new birth. After I experienced this state (which I will describe in the next chapter), everything felt brand new, as though I now had a totally changed mind and a new level of vital energy. Even my physical body no longer felt the same as before. This change proved to be a reversal that could not be undone or turned off. I felt as though I had been converted into a newly made product of better quality. This new state showed me clearly that the soul is the master of our entire existence. Prior to this realization, our individual existence is based on the control of our illusory self, the ego. But from this point on we think, act, and decide entirely from a different perspective.

Our illusionary ego doesn't drop out completely, of course, since it continues to function as needed by our real Self. As noted earlier, the ego is a survival mechanism that helps us function in the world. Yet just as everything else has been transformed internally during realization, after achieving a samadhi state the ego matures and transforms, as well. It understands its new role, sheds many of its selfish tendencies, and becomes subservient to God. Your system calls on it only when it is needed, and it does not exert the power it used to. You may feel, as I did, that from this point on the ego is working for someone else, who is directing everything. Suddenly there is a drastic shift in perception and in our attitude toward life in general.

Immediately after realization of the Self, the most difficult adjustment I had to make was regarding the way I perceived everyday life. Suddenly things seemed so impermanent and so temporary that I felt as though I did not belong here anymore. It felt strange to watch people around me going through so much suffering, stress, and frustration and continually battling with life while I seemed to be merely observing it all. It was as though time had suddenly stopped for me while it continued moving for everyone else. I felt as if I were no longer a part of the daily struggle they were all going through, neither dragging my past along nor anticipating the future. I was just moving without any specific plan or agenda, and other people's concerns had no impact on me.

At first this was truly disturbing, as everything looked empty and hopeless, and I felt as though the spice of life had evaporated and I had nothing to look forward to except *being*. I started to think that if this was what Self-realization and knowing the Truth was all about, I did not want it. I wanted to return all of it as if I were dealing with an item that I had just bought in some store and didn't like. I took each day as it came, with absolutely no motivation. Celebrations or special days, such as birthdays and anniversaries, did not seem special anymore. Each was just another day, another episode of doing whatever one is expected to do. I also began to question my feeling of detachment. I believed that enlightenment was supposed to make you more compassionate toward other people and to feel "one with all life," as it said in the books I had read. And yet I felt none of that sense of union with others. Still, when I saw someone suffering, I did feel compelled to do what I could do to help that person physically, emotionally, or financially. The simple fact that you don't feel emotionally caught up in people's suffering doesn't mean that you don't feel compassion and the desire to help relieve their suffering.

It is not as simple as that, of course, nor is it in our control to decide at what stage of spiritual evolution we will be, or when and where we will attain the Truth. We go through a process as the soul completes its inner journey, fulfilling all experiences and arriving at its final point. For a long time life felt like a drama (which in reality it is) in which I was like an actor playing without any real connection or conviction. I lost interest in my body, which I saw as merely a vehicle to get things done or something that is always present yet is no longer part of me. This feeling was so strong at times that I believed I would be here on earth for just a little longer before I left. What else was there to do? And why hang around now that the realization of Self had been accomplished? This went on for almost a year. My priorities had changed and all the thrill or excitement had gone. Planning or indulging in anything related to the future no longer had any relevance. Money, jewelry, or anything that I once considered precious had absolutely no value. From this point onward money had only one purpose as far as I was concerned: to be used efficiently with a determination to help others who were less fortunate, rather than on so many nonessentials.

When it came to buying anything, I would rather manage with what I had than look for something new. My daughter often said that we should go shopping and get new things that she thought I should have for the house. My responses irritated her, because I would say, "I have enough and we can make do with what we have. There's no need for new purchases." When she questioned the idea of making do with older things, I wasn't able to explain my state of mind, so in the end I often indulged her just to please her. I knew deep down that everything had changed so much, and now this game of life seemed so temporary. If I was here just for a while longer, why did I need to accumulate more objects?

Unfortunately, I realized I was indirectly influencing my family with this attitude. At times my husband said that I had become a "killjoy" because I never showed excitement over anything, and that made me feel bad. I didn't think that what I was going through should affect my loved ones, so I tried hard to snap out of it. I made an effort to indulge myself in the same simple pleasures that my family enjoyed, like buying new clothes or eating out. None of those things held any excitement for me, but I did my best to appear enthusiastic.

Over time, however, I learned that this play could be enjoyable and interesting if approached with a different attitude. Ultimately the knowledge we receive through realization can be integrated into everyday life, and that makes it easier to continue in spite of all the changes that have taken place. All the confusion, the months of feeling "spacey" and disoriented because of the purification process, finally subsided. Once we reach this stage there is no longer an "I" that needs to meditate. The Self has subsumed the ego, and so there is no longer any need to sit and meditate in any special way. You can meditate anywhere, at any time of the day or night. It could be in the noisiest place or while traveling, showering, or sitting in a waiting room. I am always meditating when I am traveling, as the time seems to go faster. Meditation comes spontaneously even when I want to rest. There is absolutely no need for effort after realization. Finally we experience contentment, as we constantly see our illuminated Self during deeper states of meditation.

This became a concern when I wanted to rest or sleep, though, because I was unable to go into my sleep mode right away. I would lie down to sleep but would feel as though I was meditating instead.

The minute I found myself in a still position without any physical movement, my consciousness automatically went to its higher dimension and remained there. It became a task to be in that unconscious sleep mode without any subjective awareness, because the meditative state had become like a new home to me. The natural tendency of my consciousness was to reside there as True Self.

After some time, though, I did learn how to separate the two. After all, deep sleep is needed for rejuvenation of the body so that it has the capacity to function fully in our day-to-day existence. Though I never needed much sleep after a certain point in my journey, I still wanted to rest at times without being conscious. There are some things the physical body simply cannot do without.

THIRTEEN

God Realization, the Turiya state, and the Experience of the Void

As I've said before, you may experience many levels of samadhi, or absorption in the Divine, on the journey to Self-realization. The problem is that each stop along the path feels so blissful that it can mislead you into believing that you've reached the end of the trail, so to speak—only to discover during a subsequent meditation that you can reach a higher state. The ultimate goal of realization is called Turiya, the point at which you at last experience the finest fabric of consciousness, the eternal oneness. Our mind gains total liberation as the esoteric realization and the wisdom harmonize and we experience complete equilibrium (bliss). Bliss does not mean we experience excitement of any kind, as some may think. What we experience is "perfect serenity," the consciousness of the Divine.

In this stage of undifferentiated awareness, the atman, or soul, merges with Paramatman, or God, to use the Sanskrit terms. In plain English, the individual human soul reunites with its Source; no space or time exists in that dimension of deep awareness. There is perception that transmits on its own without any perceiver. The experiential knowledge of Truth we possess at this dimension is unquestionable. The subjective stillness or void of Turiya is quite different from the deep-sleep state as I described it in the previous chapter. In deep sleep we are essentially unconscious, whereas in the Turiya state we are fully conscious of the ultimate reality of pure Being. It is as if the river finally has merged completely with the ocean. The molecules of water that made up the river are still there, but they are now participating in the infinitude of the ocean. Finally the evolutionary journey of the soul has been completed and it reestablishes a natural connection with its Source, the infinite all-pervading consciousness.

The individual knower and the infinite Known become one, and as a result we are *awareness* itself; we are *that*—as in the famous phrase from the Upanishads, "Thou art that." This awareness is beyond any duality, and the intense feeling of bliss derives from the joy of our individualized soul reuniting with its Source. This is the end point of the process of evolving from matter to body to soul. Soul has completed its journey, passing through all seven planes of consciousness and culminating in the oneness of God. For that reason we often use the term *God realization,* meaning that our consciousness has ascended to union with the Divine.

As we attune our consciousness with Divine Consciousness, right understanding takes place. We directly experience the all-pervading awareness that constitutes the entire universe. The seven planes of consciousness are correlated with the seven chakras. Consciousness first dwells in the lower three chakras, where the mind is immersed in worldliness—family, sex, money, power, and self-image—without any high ideals or pure thoughts. When consciousness moves to the fourth chakra at the heart region, we begin to glimpse a spiritual awareness, in which we experience unconditional love, compassion, and forgiveness. Our mind no longer runs after worldly pleasures. As it advances to the fifth chakra, in the throat region, consciousness is freed from all ignorance and becomes absorbed with godly topics and activities. We tend to show interest mainly in subjects relating to God and may grow impatient if any worldly topic is discussed. At the sixth chakra, the command center located between the eyebrows, the mind becomes still and one-pointed; thoughts become quiet, and intuitive knowledge develops. We are immersed in Divine Consciousness. Finally, when consciousness reaches the seventh chakra at the top of the head, the seat of higher awareness, it goes into samadhi; the individualized divinity, or Self, merges with its Source, and we realize oneness with God.

An in-depth knowledge that comes at this point from an intuitive source simply rests as perfect awareness. The kind of knowledge we gain at this ultimate stage of the journey cannot be compared with the kind we get from our ego-based existence or through the senses. It feels as though all the learning we have attained through our senses until then suddenly has no significance at all. The ultimate knowledge of who we are is beyond any understanding that we get from our limited intellect. A glimpse of this union is enough to remove all normal mental and emotional limitations. When I reached this level, I felt that there was nothing else I needed to learn. Books, titles, positions, and educational degrees all seemed meaningless and no longer fazed me. What I acquired intuitively was beyond anything that anyone could teach me. The greatest teachers have experienced this state themselves, and they can help lead you toward it, but they cannot take you there. You have to take that last step by yourself, in faith. In my case it felt utterly complete, and with it came utmost satisfaction. At this level, the mind merges with its Source, and the peace and calmness experienced cannot be translated into any language. This may be what St. Paul meant when he wrote about "the peace of God that surpasses all understanding" (Phil. 4:7).

I have come to see that intelligence in general is of two kinds. Intuitive, divine intelligence or knowledge is different from common intelligence, which is born of the senses and allows us to see the world logically. A higher intelligence or intuitive knowledge originates from the cosmic intelligence, or inner self. To attain this and realize the Truth, one need not be highly intelligent or have advanced degrees. A simple person can experience the Self and attain this knowledge intuitively. On the other hand, a highly intelligent, educated person who has attained knowledge through the senses can fail to know the ultimate Truth. Common intelligence is good and is needed to survive in this world; however, our higher purpose is to attain our true knowledge through Self-realization. This can only be experienced and cannot be studied objectively. Dr. Minott W. Lewis, a disciple of Yogananda, put it this way: "Those who meditate deeply understand many things that purely intellectual men are unable to comprehend."[1]

I feel that most people who invest their entire life in intellectual learning are not satisfied, nor do they gain any fulfillment. In their case, knowledge is sense-driven and does not come through intuition. Intuitive knowledge we attain only through meditation and it is pure knowing without the help of our intellect or senses.

I would like to explain being in this dimension in a bit more detail. Prior to reaching this point I literally felt as though I was in deep sleep, yet totally conscious and observing everything that was happening. The illumined consciousness that I experienced as inner light, or the radiance of Self, was not as heightened as it had been before, but I felt something deeper that is beyond consciousness. As I continued, the energy ascended into the utmost subtle region, and I felt an intense spinning and steady pressure at the top of my head, in the area of the crown chakra. The heightened state of focus and concentration was intense yet extremely relaxing, although not through any effort of mine.

At the same time, I felt a shift had taken place, specifically in my ears, as if all of a sudden I had become completely deaf and my mind had gone absolutely soundless. This was the first time throughout my years of intensive meditation that I felt this type of silence. It was as if I had entered a room and the door was shut so tightly behind me that not even a minute amount of air could pass through. In this dimension the mind finally goes on pause, and even the leftover thoughts that had continued passing through my conscious mind during my previous stages of transport disappeared altogether. I felt light and totally relaxed as I entered into the final layer of pure bliss.

Immediately after I entered this ecstasy of expanded emptiness, or nothingness, there appeared a clear light, a bright golden sphere surrounding an opal-blue sphere (as I described at the beginning of chapter 1). The light eventually faded away and the field appeared the color of the sky at dusk, and I was also part of it. In time my awareness increased and expanded in all directions, and I felt completely merged into this nothingness. The precise character of these experiences can't be explained in words, other than to say that I had no doubt this represented our inner Divinity revealing itself as the ultimate primordial state from which all creation springs and into which it eventually merges again. Every cell or molecule of my being seemed to have surrendered.

Once you reach this field, nothing disturbs the stillness or interferes with its peace. I remember once when I was meditating in my backyard, where I now have all my meditation sessions. The weather was warm and sunny, but after a while clouds suddenly veiled the sun and I felt a strong wind, as if a storm were about to come. I sat still, unconcerned, and continued with my meditation. Finally the wind grew even stronger and louder, yet I never felt disturbed internally. It was merely as though something had passed through without touching the inner core of my being in any way.

Once I was able to achieve the samadhi state, which took me less than ten minutes, absolutely nothing bothered me. My energy climbed quickly to the crown chakra as though it were in its permanent home, and I became immersed in that higher state. Now, after every meditation I was able to stay in my quietude, in control of when and how long I wanted to be there before I returned to normal body consciousness.

From this point, as noted earlier, I had the ability to move the inner energy to any location I wanted with ease. Sometimes, out of curiosity, I experimented with moving my inner energy to the chakras at will, fully feeling the vibration and activity of each one in turn. I was, in effect, playing around and testing how much power and control I had. Feeling this chakra activity during my meditation was proof that everything was perfect and I was fully in control.

During a typical session, I would sit and wait until the familiar light of a bright golden sphere surrounding an opal-blue sphere appeared in my field of vision, indicating the sight of the Divine. I was always cognitively aware of its appearance. Then I would feel a strong current of energy rushing up my spine, from the base to my head, with great force. This rush of energy felt heavy right before I became completely absorbed in samadhi. At this point the individualized Self and the Supreme were completely merged as one. It felt as though the Divine came and gave me a big hug, as if to say, "*Now you are finally home.*" As I was absorbed totally in the unconditioned state of oneness, the vision of the Divine appeared as the final proof of the inner guide that we all have within us. It is the ultimate Guru that guides all of us in this existence. I always found great satisfaction and completeness just being in that presence.

After some time, I would revert back to my normal waking state of sense consciousness, completing my meditation. But I usually did not return to my normal state until I felt satisfied and had enjoyed the bliss sufficiently, seeing the inner light steadily for some time, and had completely merged into the void. Regardless how blissful it was for me, I knew I could not stay there too long even if I wanted to, as I was destined to get back to my form. But the duration varied with each meditation. Sometimes it took a longer or shorter time to reach that point, but the time never mattered to me.

I noticed many times that, after I went through this process, my eyes did not open right away. I waited until all the energy was evenly distributed to my whole system before I reverted to the plane of my normal consciousness, which often took some time. Having experienced the void, I felt so free that I no longer needed to follow rules and restrictions or stick to the regimen that I had followed before. I was home now, and all the struggle and effort was finished, as I experienced an inexplicable freedom from all the day-to-day pressures, emotions, and stress of life. When you reach this state, you have drawn so much energy from the Infinite that you also require less food and less sleep, and the type of food you eat does not have the impact on your system that it once did. When you live in the Self as the Self, you require very little to sustain day-to-day living. This explains why I am rarely tired or hungry now. I am always with full of energy that never seems to deplete. As Ramana Maharshi says, "Once you attain illumination, it will make less difference what you eat, as, on a great fire, it is immaterial what fuel is added."[2]

After realization I still continued my regular morning meditation, even if it was just for a little while each day. It felt good to leave this sensory consciousness and enter the space of expanded awareness, that dimension of spaciousness, "the Absolute." It was different, though, since it was no longer a struggle and I didn't need to follow a particular discipline regarding when and how long to meditate. In a sense I was always meditating, but somehow I still preferred sitting in a particular place, as that seemed to provide greater satisfaction. There was enjoyment in just sitting, seeing, and being the illuminated Self that merges back to the Source. To be able at last to experience that ecstasy was truly a gift.

However, the sensations of heat and vibration remained the same, which was uncomfortable at times. I became accustomed to living with expanded consciousness and dealing with the increased inner fire while it continued to integrate with my system. From this point onward my body was never as before. My entire body continued emitting higher temperatures than usual, with an overwhelming amount of energy. In order to keep it manageable, I had to engage daily in some kind of vigorous exercise, in addition to what I normally do.

As a result I no longer could tolerate hotter climates and preferred cooler living conditions, which better suited my system.

The Golden Sphere, or Divine Light

Whenever I close my eyes now, I am able to see the bright golden sphere surrounding an opal-blue sphere, indicating the divine presence, even when I am still involved with bodily activities. This continues every day, as I am constantly fluctuating between relative sense consciousness and the infinite, supreme Self. It is especially easy to see the light early in the morning just before waking up, because I have been there all night in deep sleep. At that early hour the senses have not yet become active and the mind is most clear and sharp. All I have to do is close my eyes and think of the Divine, and the light appears right away.

I've said that we are always with our formless divinity in deep sleep but are unaware of it. However, I can also see the light at night, just before falling asleep or when I am in my resting mode. It is as though the Divine himself comes and greets me before I start the day and says good night before I end the day. To be with the divine presence within and be able to see the light at will comes only after experiencing the deeper dimension of Turiya, since consciousness remains steadfast as it merges into the pure energy of nothingness.

I take the appearance of the inner Divinity as a blessed opportunity and literally speak with it by saying, "Good morning" and "What are we doing today?" This may sound funny, but the Divinity responds and helps me by giving me a clear perspective on the day, as everything is being told by "it." This has become my daily routine and I never have any particular agenda. I know everything I need to do just by being there and looking at the light for fifteen minutes or so prior to getting up. This gives me an added boost of energy before I awaken fully and revert to normal sense consciousness. Any morning discomfort disappears after I am with the light for those few minutes. As I focus on the light, the inner energy comes into balance and seems to harmonize itself and recover its equilibrium.

Among the many positive changes that I experienced after realization, I also observed a shift in my attitude whenever I was agitated by a discussion or argument. In those situations I now go to that expanded dimension of pure Self where I enter a calm, silent region of utmost peace. This profound center of peace seems to lie beneath and persist throughout any negative situation, keeping me in harmony at all times. In general, when we reach this point of realization, we don't appear to feel excitement, surprise, or even joy. At last there is no room for doubt or any confusion about who we are. Instead we feel a strong conviction that everything that is happening is real and true. We no longer need to seek confirmation, because we have seen and felt this truth. We know that this is who we are and that the Divine resides within each and every living creature. It is as simple as that.

I've said that I passed through several different levels of samadhi on my way to realization. Some of the states have terms in Sanskrit that may help to explain them, although they may seem a bit technical. During *savikalpa samadhi,* for instance, one's consciousness does not lose its identity but does temporarily dissolve into God. As a number of spiritual masters have pointed out, the body enters a trancelike state while the mind is conscious only of the Divine within and is not conscious of the external world.

By contrast, in the state of *nirvikalpa samadhi,* which is a bit more intense, we unfold to the infinite expansion of nothingness and lose our bodily fixation temporarily. For a short interval the life force is withdrawn from our senses completely and the body appears motionless. However, after experiencing this bliss we may feel that we still have a hold on the form. Even at this highest nondual state, the Self retains some degree of individualized consciousness without completely dissolving into the Absolute. The depth of this loss of physical sensation varies for each individual, and from time to time with the same individual.

At some moments I felt absolutely no body consciousness, while at other times I felt that only certain parts of my body were "missing," including my arms, legs, and face—and I didn't know where they were. I went through many variations of this plane, but having some prior knowledge made it easier for me to handle the experience without much agitation. I also learned that the longer we stay at the level of nirvikalpa samadhi, the longer it takes to come back to our normal sense consciousness. The first time I experienced losing control over my body, right after coming back from almost two hours of deep meditation, I was not able to stay in that state for long. It is a shaky feeling, as if we are attached to the body and at the same time not attached to it. As many ancient seers have stated, the body cannot function for long without the sense of Self anyway, especially when one is destined to return to body consciousness and be active in the world, as I was. Perhaps some can permanently establish themselves in that state. The parts of the body feel and look dead; my hands felt heavy, dropped down without any life, and appeared swollen. Once when I tried to put on my bracelet, it wouldn't fit because my fingers and hand were so swollen. On another occasion after meditating for two hours, when

I tried to stand up I fell down and lost control of both my legs and hands. It felt as though there was no strength or life in them, and my head was still spinning because normal feelings had not returned to the system completely. To counter this I learned to sit in my chair for some time, until I was fully conscious. I often took at least ten to twenty minutes before getting back to my normal tasks. I would also end each meditation with at least five to eight minutes of pranayama, so that the prana would get distributed evenly to my system before I tried to stand up again.

I often felt extremely cold in spite of the moderate climate. Sometimes I experienced such stillness while in that state of infinite timelessness that I found it impossible to believe I even existed. This state is so far beyond duality that our accustomed way of thinking totally disappears. While you are in this plane, the outgoing and incoming breath becomes balanced to such an extent that you feel as if you are hardly breathing—or perhaps not breathing at all. In the past, when I went into deeper states of meditation, my inhalations and exhalations became very short, but at this point my breath totally stopped for a short period. This state is called *kumbhaka* in Sanskrit, and as with samadhi, there are several different levels, or modes, of breathlessness. Everything stands still and we experience supreme tranquility without having to do anything. The life energy gets switched off from our senses and muscles automatically, making it seem that everything is dead and without sensation.

My body became so totally relaxed that I was unaware of it. It was as if every muscle had released its life force and all the vital energy had been drained out. That may explain why my body felt cold and lifeless at these times, as if no organs were functioning. The deep peace I felt when merged in that emptiness, resting as awareness, was rarely disturbed. The Mother explained this by saying that the body is "like hundreds of combined entities or multiple entities unaware of each other, yet all harmonized by something deeper which they don't know."[3]

We must experience our individualized divinity, the illuminated Self within us, before merging back to the void. It is a sequential and progressive journey. Once we gain the ultimate transcendental knowledge of oneness from that emptiness, we need no other confirmation. The wisdom comes from a totally different and fully awakened perception that we attain only after experiencing the Turiya state. There is a true intelligence and a sense of knowing that arises from within or by just *being*. As Nisargadatta Maharaj says, "Wisdom is knowing I am nothing."[4]

Along with confidence, we feel a sense of equanimity and a quality of peace that comes from knowing that we are finally home. It is as if every cell and organ, every mental and physical function has synchronized perfectly. All we have to do, as the great teachers have always said, is just be in the moment.

Equanimity

I did not fully understand what equanimity meant until I started to experience it. Once you are realized, you do not feel any different whether you are experiencing pain, sorrow, or joy. When you are one with the higher consciousness, you live in the Self, as the Self, unattached to all activities and their results. This means living within a different plane of consciousness that has a higher vibrational frequency. We are no longer in our normal plane of sense consciousness. It means being in constant harmony with all happenings in the universe and carrying this state of equanimity throughout every situation and in dealings with other people. It is a unique type of attitude that we carry toward life in general, with that utmost evenness. Realization helps us gain mastery over our mind so that we are always at peace, regardless of any disturbances that may take place around us. This kind of self-control springs from a state of mind, not an act of will. We react to pleasant and unpleasant situations with the same perfect balance, harmony, and equilibrium. We do not get overly excited nor overly sad with any situation, and we are able to handle everything with utmost calm and ease. When you display this kind of attitude, some people may mistake you for being indifferent about worldly happenings. It is not that realized individuals do not have any emotions or feelings, just that they don't let them have any lasting impact. They have emotions but don't become emotional.

One advantage of not being ruled by emotions is that when you view all beings impartially, freed from personal likes and dislikes, decision making becomes easier. It became easier for me to avoid getting worked up and stressed out during disagreements with other people, or to hold grudges for a long period of time. Even today when anger comes over me, I react to it at the moment just as anyone would, but then it immediately subsides. There is no residual agitation that tends to build upon itself, creating more negative thoughts. Although at times I had to act as if I were excited or sad just for the sake of others, I had become a nonexcitable entity. There was absolutely nothing that could damage my inner peace. This is the equanimity that we gain from being with our true nature.

Since being realized, I have not experienced either overexcitement or extreme sadness in any situation. I don't run toward sense objects nor do I take myself away from them. Most of the time my mind remains peaceful, accepting everything as it is. When my mother died, for example, her death did not disturb me unduly. She had suffered from health challenges most of her life. I realized that it was her time to go, and I was at peace with this fact. Prior to her death, I knew that she was going to pass away in few days. I was fully aware of everything taking place in her system. I saw that her kundalini had been awakened involuntarily and I knew it was time for her soul to leave that body.

As mentioned before, the dormant life energy that is within all of us will awaken on only two occasions—when we are ready to reach enlightenment and when we are leaving the body and returning to Source. The second scenario represents the last opportunity to realize our Self prior to dying and having to go through reincarnation yet again. Yet many people miss it through ignorance of what is happening, since it is a very brief encounter and they are simply not conscious of it. They are still attached to the illusionary material world and see death with anxiety instead of understanding, with gratitude, that we are with our Source at that moment.

Pain and Suffering

"So many of the problems and troubles we run into are created by our mistaking for permanent that which is actually impermanent." So says the Dalai Lama,[5] explaining succinctly the major misconception of this life. That is in part why the knowledge that cosmic consciousness expresses within us comes as a shock when we achieve Self-realization. Normally we live completely absorbed with our illusionary state of being, unaware that anything to do with the gross body and mind is not permanent, and so will change, disintegrate, and ultimately cease to be. This misunderstanding creates suffering, worry, and pain. Once we have the vision of our Self, all the suffering subsides.

The way I see it, the Divine has created the mortal form of body and mind to let us experience, feel, and do everything in this manifestation. The body has the capacity to address all physical, mental, and emotional imbalances, to heal, and to maintain harmony. Whenever our vital energy or life force is depleted by physical, emotional, and mental exhaustion we suffer or worry. Yet the body can take care by itself by tapping into its natural storehouse of cosmic energy lying within us. We have merely to learn how to use that supply of energy for a healthy living. When this pranic flow is disturbed or gets distributed unevenly in our system due to irregularities in lifestyle, then we are vulnerable to suffering and disease. If we maintain equilibrium of our vital energy within, we will overcome any illness. We can increase our vital energy and align our Self with that higher energy field to eradicate any type of suffering. We can bring back that harmony by listening to it in silence. This is what I believe and practice.

I have not encountered any major health issues in my life, except for a few occasional common colds, and after I attained my realization I was able to control even those. I feel there will always be suffering, agitation and difficulty when we look for happiness in the external pursuit of wealth, power or acknowledgment, instead of by knowing and realizing our inner self. We also suffer when we become too attached to materialism from an innate belief in the permanency of things. I am not saying that deep spiritual dedication and attaining realization render us immune to sickness or suffering. Most people, including realized spiritual masters, have faced difficulties of sickness and, ultimately, death. But I do believe that we probably could alleviate some of our pain with a strong sense of trust, belief, and self-control from within. Realization and attainment of a higher state of consciousness gives us tools with which to awaken our inner strength to control imbalances and to be able to keep the whole system in harmony, as we are more aware of our inner self. One should be able to put these tools into practice when necessary.

Fear of Death

Only after experiencing the nondual state of our True Self, or the divinity within, can we understand the meaning of "death while living." But what does this phrase actually mean, and why do we fear death?

Fear comes primarily for two related reasons. The first is that we don't understand what death amounts to, and the second is simply that the life we are leading is going to end. The prospect of almost any ending, such as the loss of a home, the death of a loved one, or the end of a personal relationship or a job, may cause fear and anxiety. But to know with certainty that one day we will no longer have this life that we have built for ourselves can be devastating. As I've mentioned, apart from the deep-sleep state, we are in contact with our inner Divinity on only two occasions. One is when the subtle body departs and the gross body is dissolved at death, and the other when we are in the highest meditative state and attain enlightenment while still living in the physical body. In both cases we end up shedding the false identification of our existence, but only the latter involves realizing the Self (Truth) while we are conscious. Because of this understanding, the fear of death vanishes when we experience a thorough awareness of the merge into the Absolute (void). Not having known or experienced this dimension beforehand is what causes fear at the prospect of death.

Although the opportunity exists to attain self-knowledge after dissolution of the body, this is not so easy to achieve. Unless we have already experienced the Self *consciously,* we will easily miss this encounter when it takes place at death. The experience must be conscious and steadfast for one to attain liberation and immortality; otherwise the cycle of birth, death, and rebirth continues. It is just such a transition to a higher state that we attain through meditation. Every time we are absorbed in the samadhi (void) of pure awareness, in a way we are dying while continuing to live in this form, because we are in direct contact with the Absolute. In meditation we have, for the first time, a definite confirmation that we are absolutely a "nothing" as opposed to being a physical part of the material universe our mind perceives. We finally realize that this inner energy is immortal and there is no such thing as death. It is simply a return to the original unmanifest state of primordial nature. We feel fear at death only if we have never consciously experienced our true nature while alive and make the mistake of identifying with the impermanent existence of the body and sense consciousness.

Losing fear of death takes some time even after enlightenment. The higher consciousness must establish completely and permanently through our conscious will. As realization deepens and matures further through continuous meditation, fear gradually disappears. In my own experience, fear lingered for some time, until I was able to identify completely with higher awareness by merging repeatedly with emptiness. It subsided only after the process of realization had been well established and integrated completely through meditating and experiencing the void repeatedly. We must maintain and continue the practice of being with the new awareness while continuing all our activities. Though the mind may fluctuate in and out at times, a sense of control will come automatically and remain in that higher plane with the feeling of peace.

FOURTEEN

The Upside and Downside of Realization

I want to emphasize again that becoming Self-realized does not mean that all of a sudden you will be leading a heavenly life without pain, suffering, or frustration. As you may have gathered by now, the transition from ordinary consciousness to permanently altered perception of reality entails any number of challenging adjustments to a difficult way of living over an extended time. Few people who have not been there can understand the significant adjustments one needs to make after attaining realization. Because it's still not a commonplace experience, it can be a challenge to assimilate with those around you once your perception of life has changed so radically. Although I had read and listened to many saints, teachers, and realized beings prior to realization, I found it odd that none of them ever talked about this aspect of the journey.

Some yogis and enlightened sages have written or said things that make achieving an enlightened state sound nothing short of delightful. But it is a misconception to believe that once you reach realization you will walk around in a permanent state of bliss, or that experiencing the nectar of deep meditation makes everything else in life taste like nectar, too. Nothing could be further from the truth. It is not always entirely harmonious, nor does our life become perfect in the way that many people may think. It would be more accurate to say that once you taste the nectar, everything else tastes terrible by comparison—and continues to taste terrible! We alternate between a lot of built-up resentments, fear, confusion, and struggle for some time, even after realization. For a long time after attaining realization I used to question whether it wouldn't be better to end my life instead of lingering and continuing the drama in this earthly form. Then I realized that ending my life would demean the whole purpose of divine cosmic play. After all, the purpose of realization is to live fully and completely, removing all the falseness that we have created for ourselves. Indeed, we are meant to use our full potentiality by experiencing all that exists with utmost peace and contentment. Until we have explored and understood living in a higher state of awareness, our journey back to the Source cannot be completed. To be honest, continuing to live in this world and doing the laundry of everyday life can feel overwhelming at times. In the beginning at least, it can seem as if the fake building we have constructed to protect us from the elements has collapsed, and now we are exposed to everything. Observing all the suffering and poverty and the day-to-day struggle of everyone seems to affect me tremendously since realization. Suddenly I began getting more involved with it all and trying to make it better for everyone but at the same time getting frustrated constantly because any amount of involvement on my part seemed simply an unsatisfying drop in the bucket.

Almost every book I've read and most of the enlightened teachers I have heard use the word *happiness* to describe the state of realization. But I don't believe such happiness exists; what I have experienced is more like an abiding contentment and peace, a sense of detachment from everything and everyone, which leaves me without worry or fear. To be able to face the world and the objects of enjoyment with that perfect indifference can be a challenge. What most people consider being happy depends on conditions and situations we perceive as being positive and favorable, and results in a state of elation that is impermanent to begin with. Happiness may depend on attaining good health and material prosperity and satisfying all one's desires. But what I am describing is a state of mind that does not carry agitation, anxiety, or stress and that maintains tranquility regardless of the surrounding conditions. Whatever is, is perfectly okay. That may include physical pain, less-than-optimal finances, or the death or suffering of loved ones. That is simply how it is; instead of "happiness," I would call it "just being."

Yet I have to acknowledge that this state of "just being" initially comes with a good deal of confusion, loneliness, distress, and boredom! Among other things, those around you may perceive you as an oddball, in part because you no longer get thrilled about the material goods this world has to offer. As I said in the previous chapter, I stopped feeling exhilaration over the things that excite most people. My daughter occasionally said that I was no longer as before, that I had become boring because I showed little interest in shopping, movies, traveling, dinner outings, and so on. My lack of interest wasn't a judgment on them but merely a fact of my new life. At least that is how I felt for a long time after my enlightenment. Don't get me wrong. I still functioned well while participating in everything that I was supposed to do, including certain obsessions and habits that continued to linger, like getting certain tasks done right away as opposed to procrastinating, not being able to sleep without exercising, reading prior to sleeping, or even simple tasks such as washing the dishes and putting them away before going to bed.

Attaining realization does not instantly set one on a smooth course, and every stage in the process has its pros and cons that we need to deal with until everything is integrated. Until then, all emotional and mental disturbances will continue to linger. The nondual wisdom that is gained must be integrated skillfully and effortlessly into our relative human existence. The Dalai Lama defines wisdom as "the ability to perceive reality along with a disposition to act in accord with right values."[1] That can be difficult for some time.

This is why, even two years after realization, I still faced up and down days, including occasional bouts of extreme depression. I suspect that the depression resulted from the radical transition from being in ecstatic transcendence, as I continued my deep meditations, to the everyday business of daily life. Emerging from a blissful few hours of meditation and returning to normal material consciousness continued to be disorienting. We should be able to abide stably with the Absolute perception of reality and the relative worldly perception so that we can continue with the given embodied existence. I had to learn to handle external life and interactions with everyone without becoming irritated and frustrated. Inward change and outward interaction must go side by side, and that can take years to accomplish. Still at times it continues to be a difficult and elaborate adjustment on my part.

Jivanmukta

St. Paul wrote in the New Testament, "And do not be conformed to this world, but be transformed by the renewing of your mind, in order to prove by you what is that good and pleasing and perfect will of God" (Romans 12:2). We should function with our full potential in this world without getting absorbed or driven by worldly things, but living with total freedom as a *jivanmukta*, as they call it in Eastern scriptures. In this state the mind is no longer chasing fulfillment through worldly pleasures.

The Sanskrit word *jivanmukta* (literally, "liberated while in the body") can be applied to anyone who has realized the Self and attained liberation from the cycle of birth, death, and rebirth while still living in human form. According to Advaita philosophy, once we attain the knowledge of Self, which is free from all limitations of time and space and objects, we no longer have to take on a new body or a particular form on earth; this is a state of existence technically called *moksha*.

Jivanmuktas appear to be in the world, but are not involved in the world. They are living in an unattached state and continuing to function for the sake of humanity without any personal gain. Though they appear to ordinary eyes to be like any ordinary happy person, their activities are different, as they have a clear understanding of their mission in life. They are categorized into many types depending on their nature and status and the priorities and activities, both worldly and spiritual, that they have set out to accomplish. Physically they demand nothing; emotionally they have no impediments; and they are intellectually brilliant, as they have no distractions or hang-ups of any kind. They do not care to remember their past, which has been erased, and they do not worry about their future because it gets taken care by itself.

Jivanmuktas dedicate their time to selfless service to humanity. Some are active in the world and others immerse themselves in God consciousness while remaining aware of their material existence. They are contented without riches or sense pleasures but are inwardly powerful and wealthy, as their wealth comes from their true nature of being. Since they are not identified with their body, mind, and senses, pleasure and pain do not have any lasting impact on them. Each one's spiritual process is unique in itself.

But being in this state raises several issues that can be difficult to comprehend or explain. Although realizing that state of heightened awareness requires years of dedication and discipline for some people, in the end that was the easy part for me. People often ask, for instance, how one integrates the shift of higher consciousness with the everyday world of life with the family. Is it possible to put into practice the resulting insights and change of consciousness on the level of mundane reality? Having experienced both levels of earthly life, I've learned how difficult it can be at times to cope with the turmoil that takes place in the typical family setting. Before you realize the Truth, you tend be get caught up in the delusive mundane life, but after realization everything looks and feels different. Those around you may have difficulty understanding the change in perspective that follows an experience of realization, and this can be frustrating for everyone. I often felt almost suffocated by the complaints and demands from those around me. At the same time I was disappointed at how long the spiritual process was taking, how overwhelming it all felt. I even began to hate the whole thing, and I couldn't understand why I was feeling this way when enlightenment is supposed to fill you with love for everyone. Instead I often wanted to drop everything and everyone and leave.

I also wondered if I had actually transcended my ego, as I had been told this is part of the process of realization. When I was in deep meditation, I felt connected to the universe and all sentient beings. But when I came back to the active world, I found it challenging to continue my roles as wife and mother, trying to deal with the minutiae of the material world by using the new energy that had emerged. For instance, I felt a most untranscendent need for my family members to adjust to my new mentality, in which I interpreted life from a spiritual point of view as opposed to one based on the senses and intellect. Sometimes my husband and children complained that I was preaching to them, and I'm sure it may have sounded like that at times. This caused misunderstanding, irritation, and frustration in the family setting.

Eventually I realized that they were right and that I could not impose my inner changes in my perception of life on others, so I cut down on my "preaching." I learned that we are totally free only when we can give complete freedom to others to be as they are. Realization doesn't give us the right to change others, because everyone is being just as they should be according to their place along their own journey. I was still growing and adapting, myself, so it was presumptuous to expect everyone else to be where I thought they should be.

The new perceptions that derive from spending time in higher states are not necessarily harmonized or synchronized completely, and so we often may not have the clarity we need to continue functioning in daily life. Each individual processes these perceptions in different ways, depending on how far they have penetrated into our mortal consciousness and stabilized the expression of the Self. This is why we need to continue with meditation, although not necessarily on the same intensive schedule as before. As our awareness continues to mature further and integrates completely, we may still feel some ups and downs even after realization.

I was fortunate in many ways that the material circumstances of my life were favorable in helping me accomplish my goal. Whether this was based on previous karma I can only guess, but it was beneficial that I found myself in a comfortable family setting as opposed to being alone.

To have gone through my transformation without the support of my husband and the comfort of my home and children might have made my journey much more arduous. I was also lucky that my spiritual development unfolded in a sequential, orderly manner. I have heard of many others for whom the path to Self-realization was abrupt, launching with a sudden shock and not following any particular order. So although I may not have had all the emotional support and understanding from my family that I would have liked, I'm grateful that I did have a materially supportive environment.

As I have explained in my earlier chapters, I experienced renunciation and detachment over a period of years before I began any disciplined practice. The dispassion I felt for ordinary life was matched by my intense passion for the Divine, and together they made my life change direction. Even my interest in meditation evolved out of my study and practice of Reiki healing, which also led to an increased desire to know the Truth through the study of scriptures, books, and association with certain realized individuals, past and present. My meeting with Amma Karunamayi now seems preordained, and happened at just the right moment in my spiritual unfolding, as she was able to shepherd me through what had begun as an intensely private practice. My development was then enhanced by her teachings and guidance and by pilgrimages that I made to sacred places in India with an intention to devote myself to deep meditation and selfless work. Finally, I was blessed with experiencing my true inner Divinity, the realization of oneness. That realization did not come easily, as should be clear from my description of the torturous challenges created by changes in consciousness along the path. And yet it all happened in the setting of my family life. As I have said numerous times, we need not go away anywhere to find Truth, because realization can take place in any given circumstance.

My husband accepted pretty much everything I did and adjusted graciously to my new life as it unfolded, yet I really don't know whether he had any clue about the inner turmoil I was going through most of the time prior to my realization—all the long meditation sessions at odd times, waking up in the middle of the night from those heat episodes, my irritable mood swings, depression, unusual eating habits, and reduced interest in social activities. Even if he did have some inkling of what I was going through, perhaps he preferred not to involve himself, as he could not have done much to help. However, in all other aspects he was supportive and cooperative and kept me in utmost comfort all through my journey. And in the end, I chose to keep the intensity of my inner battle a secret from everyone except my guru. I knew it would be impossible for anyone else, including my husband, to imagine what I was going through, since they had not yet experienced Self-realization. So in some way they were better off not knowing. Of course, much had already been written about realization, but in order to know the truth of such a process one must experience it personally. The most frustrating aspect of the whole process was that I could not communicate it to anyone who had not experienced it. I missed discussing my concerns with someone who would understand them in their complexity, but could not until I visited my teacher, who was the only one to whom I could open up fully. But apart from this and other hurdles that I had to face due to my transformation, I had no complaints about anything else in my life.

Nevertheless, I used to wonder if it would be better to be a man in this state, but I eventually realized it would not make any difference whether one was a woman or man, monk or nun. My daily tasks not only were boring, but also felt like an imposition at times, as I was functioning with a different energy level. On occasion my husband got frustrated when I was no longer carrying out certain tasks properly or conscientiously, in part because I had become more prone to procrastination and forgetfulness. When questioned, I often got irritated and defensive because I no longer wanted to continue doing those things, and my tendency to put off and forget them became a habit.

I wanted to resign from this job of wife and mother and have someone else take over and set me free to attend to what interested me. I felt that all the rules and regulations that we set for ourselves no longer applied, because they were manmade and conditioned to begin with. I had my own way of thinking and doing things, and I'm sure this irritated a few people. Preparing meals became a nuisance that I had to get out of as quickly as possible, since I considered it to be the biggest waste of time. Eating became my last priority. As mentioned earlier, my food consumption declined sharply. With the new energy I felt, and having no hunger most of the time, I began to be concerned about the extent to which food is at the center of most social life; almost everything we do revolves around food, including our social activities, entertainment, and celebrations.

This disinterest created an almost frightening situation regarding food. I certainly did not want to eat when my system did not require it. But to avoid eating, or to find credible ways to say no without being conspicuous, was often tricky. At social gatherings I became an oddball and a target of attention, and I was at a loss how to explain all this to others. Yet the fact remained that being absorbed in the Self gave me such tremendous energy that I did not need to eat frequently. Through meditation we draw energy from the Cosmic Source and retain it within the body. Where there is no movement or activity all the energy remains inward, and as a result we require less food and less sleep. The spectrum of consciousness we carry after realization is no longer the same as before. I felt no hunger most of the time, and one simple meal a day was plenty. For a long time after I attained realization, only fruit and fruit juices would agree with my stomach. There were many times when I could go without food all day.

Regardless of the way I was feeling, I fulfilled my responsibilities without any complaints, more out of obligation than desire. I avoided all the attention, arguments, discussions, and explanations by pretending that everything was fine.

I often did not want to talk to anyone and found it difficult to converse even with my own family members. I became irritated and angry with simple things, believing I no longer belonged in these circumstances, and did not want to continue with this kind of life.

Perhaps this is the reason many enlightened beings choose to live by themselves in secluded venues without having to deal with family, friends, or relatives. Though I felt at times that this would be the perfect solution, I could never put it into practice and actually leave others behind. I always felt a deep responsibility toward my family and didn't believe I could abandon them. Eventually I would learn how to integrate everything from a practical point of view and have the best of both worlds.

This sense of conflict made me feel so hopeless that I often cried. Out of frustration I became argumentative and assertive and wanted everyone to understand things from my perspective. Although others may have construed this as egotistical or arrogant, my intention was never to project those attitudes. After experiencing the Truth through realization, I became straightforward and to the point in my communication. I felt no need to hesitate or sugarcoat anything for convenience and was not concerned with the consequences of what I said. My tendency to avoid people, places, and certain situations increased. I would stay away from places if there was any possibility of confrontation or disagreement with others, because those feelings now manifested as some sort of physical discomfort in my system. In general I tried to avoid controversial topics or discussions in day-to-day life, and I found the most difficult task was to talk to or deal with people who viewed life differently than I did. I especially found it difficult to communicate with some who projected a demeanor that carried excessive pride and arrogance. I am aware everyone carries false ego, but certain people tend to project it a bit more.

It took an effort on my part to manage this, as I do recognize that everyone lives with a particular perception of life, to which they are entitled. Still, my tolerance level had decreased tremendously for any discussions of politics, gossip, or chitchat regarding who owns nicer or more expensive houses, cars, or other possessions.

As I've said, after experiencing the Truth one becomes detached from everything and everyone, yet one often needs to appear engaged in order to blend in and do whatever it takes to manage the situation. The fact that I no longer suffered any intense emotional impact from the sickness or death of those around me or from other catastrophic happenings of life appeared peculiar to most people. I was questioned and confronted unceasingly about this by my own family members. They frequently considered me to be some kind of stone-like, unemotional being, and so I often had to justify my demeanor.

I once asked Amma about this and she said, "These things would still exist because the environment we are in is not conducive with the consciousness we carry after the realization. Therefore, all human attributes, including anger, frustration, and irritation, will still be there even after realization. This includes the feeling of not wanting to be here any longer. But they do not bind us, and so they simply come and go."

When I asked her if these attributes and emotions bother her, she smiled and said no. From this I understood that she is on a different plane from just about everyone else. She came here as an avatar, pure energy that takes a bodily form in order to help all sentient beings, and so can't really be compared with other Self-realized beings. Avatars come to earth for a purpose and leave when they finish what they are supposed to do. There is so much more about these supreme beings that I don't understand completely.

As time went on, I chose to associate only with those who exemplified the same ideals as I did and practiced them in their daily lives. I never waivered in the things that I wanted to do and never looked for approval or consent from anyone, including those who were close to me. Instead of involving myself with routine issues and day-to-day tasks, I now tended to focus on a specific goal, usually some type of service or something more creative. New ideas, new ways of living, new thoughts all arise naturally from being in the state of expanded consciousness. That enhanced creativity of mind may be the reason I started to write this book even though I had never written a book before.

At the same time, few of the people who knew me believed it was possible that I could have reached a higher plane of consciousness, and this became a delicate situation to handle. I had no way to explain the complete transformation that had taken place in me to anyone who did not have knowledge or experience of Self-realization, even those who were closest to me, and so I felt uncomfortable talking about this. How can you convince family members or friends that you have reached a higher state of consciousness without making it sound offensive, even delusional? I am aware now that this understanding is not often believable to anyone who has no inkling of what Self-actualization is. This may be why some skeptics hate the whole concept of higher consciousness and its values. Yet now that I was aware of my true nature, I had no need to present a false identity to please others. Nor did I feel it is necessary to try to achieve something or make an impact in the world, or to accumulate disciples. I was comfortable just being, and carrying out the routine activities of daily life with the intent of bringing quality to everything I did. Once a person has attained realization, the old self disappears and is replaced by a new understanding of Truth that changes everything. This is not something we should feel proud to have achieved, but simply the way we are all intended to live, without any limitations or restrictions and with our full energetic potential.

And so I tried my best to balance the apparent contradiction that, although I had achieved a state of consciousness that was supposed to make me feel at one with all other beings, I still tended to speak in ways that might alienate them. I was aware that the inner confidence that comes with the knowledge of realization could be perceived by some as egotistic or arrogant, but as far as I was concerned, I was simply stating the facts. As Gandhi once said, "The only tyrant I accept in this world is the 'still small voice' within me. And even though I have to face the prospect of being a minority of one, I humbly believe I have the courage to be in such a hopeless minority"[2]

In order to survive in this world we all live with an ego that is of a different nature prior to realization. After we experience the Truth we carry a new mentality. It could be seen as egotistical, but it comes from knowing that the Truth is genuine, and acts as a force that brings positive results. Further, this level of energy and inner confidence is a great help when we want to teach or guide others. After enlightenment, everything we do arises from that inner source instead of from our illusory ego, the driving force that propelled our life before realization. This is the deeper truth behind the saying of Francis Bacon that "knowledge is power"; the knowledge of your inner self infuses you with extraordinary power. That knowledge also gives you the confidence that what you are radiating is genuine. The old version of ego-driven self disappears because you no longer need that to survive.

All prior curiosity and the questions you once sought to answer by following other enlightened souls, participating in devotional activities, and visiting spiritual places simply go away. The reason is simple: once you have experienced that nondual state about which you were so desperately curious, it is as though you have ceased being a student and have obtained an advanced degree. From this point on, there is not much difference between all realized individuals, although each one's life purpose and intention differs. Whatever the surface distinctions, a mutual respect and deep friendship for one another will always remain. I have always held in high regard and had a deep appreciation and gratitude for those teachers who assist individuals who are on the path to reach their goals.

Among the changes in my attitudes and behaviors following realization was that I no longer felt the need to maintain a special shrine area for meditation. Now any outdoor, open environment was perfect. Nature became my personal shrine, as I had always preferred to meditate outside, anyway. I became my own temple; I could call on the Divine at will, at any time, as it resided within me. I had never had an overwhelming desire to perform worship activities, such as chanting and *puja*, but now I lost interest in them altogether. And so, having a specific place with statues or pictures of divine representations did not carry weight any longer—again, because I had experienced the Divine within me. The system that has been established for centuries, in which individuals pray in specific places, such as temples, churches, synagogues, or any special spiritual location, seemed unnecessary and totally lost its attractiveness. I realize that my attitude about this is at odds with the practice of many realized beings, including my own beloved teacher, but as I've said before there is no one way that realization manifests.

The drive to learn from spiritual books that are such a part of the early stages of the journey—fueled by endless curiosity and mental restlessness—also tends to vanish after realization has been achieved. There is no volition any more. That "need to know" that was so intense before disappears completely. In the end it becomes evident that to be able to function in day-to-day life requires readjustments in every aspect of living. Initially the mind vacillates between the old way of being ruled by ego and living according to our true nature; even after realization, certain fixations and misconceptions linger for some time. One's personality does not change at all, yet one's way of thinking changes. Realized individuals may look the same and do the same as everyone else, but who they are is different in every aspect of their lives. They function without attachment to or involvement with anything in particular. As you desire nothing after realization, you are left to contribute to the world in your own way with full enthusiasm and without pressure.

When we reach a higher level of perception, our sense of compassion and unconditional love rise naturally and genuinely, and we feel a deep peace and joy from within at the thought of helping others. There is no selfish motive or expectation behind expressing the kindness we feel. Before realization, we all love helping our close relatives and friends because we want to be liked or recognized or to be thanked by them. This level of kindness is driven by ego and springs from attachment and grasping. The desire to help those to whom we have no kinship or friendship, by contrast, comes from our heart and is caused by an inner drive operating with a different force. Enlightened beings feel a powerful desire to be of service to others, to make life better for all sentient beings; indeed, that becomes a priority.

After realization my concern for other human beings multiplied exponentially, along with the desire to use my money and resources for good. The increased pranic energy compels us to engage in more altruistic activities, and the intuitive knowledge regarding how to help is directed by the higher Source, so that we can experience true gratification. It's a blessing just to be given the opportunity to be of compassionate service. As I see it, even to help, we need two main ingredients: first, a sound mentality or attitude of wanting to help; and second, the capability or resources that allow us to help. Although it is ideal to have both, we may not all have the material resources. But I do feel we gain the right mindset after attaining realization—and with that alone we can try to make a difference.

The downside of this fervor to be of service can be a feeling that we have much to accomplish and little time; this made me even more reluctant to waste any more time and energy on day-to-day tasks.

The most important positive aspect of being permanently established in the nondual state is the ability to overcome just about anything. You become more attuned to the inner signaling of the chakra system and are better able to control any issues within the gross body, including the mind. Being able to move that new energy easily increases your ability either to heal or to make discriminative decisions. As the new consciousness takes over, your intuitive power and spiritual strength increase and you tend to remain in equanimity. The stability and depth of realization mature and deepen further as you continue with meditation. Only then will you be able to approach the world with humility and gratitude, and to surrender with total dependence on the Divine.

Reaching higher consciousness does not mean that you need to give up everything, however, or deny all the pleasures, thrills, and delights that life offers. It also does not necessarily mean you must behave in a particular manner and avoid doing certain things. On the contrary, it is about how well you live in the world without being attached, and accepting life as it is. There's a Tibetan Buddhist prayer that goes, in part, "And may all live in equanimity, without too much attachment and too much aversion, and live believing in the equality of all that lives."

And over time, the positives outweigh the temporary negative issues. Eventually, the higher state of our consciousness helps us to experience every aspect of life as something meaningful and sacred, which encompasses caring for our physical body as the temple of the spirit. Still, we have to be patient until the full integration takes place. How well we adjust to these changes also depends on our tolerance, courage, and discriminative wisdom. As the latter increases, we are able to set boundaries for ourselves without hesitation and make decisions with confidence. This is based on the level of awareness that we gain from continuously being established in our True Self.

Among other positive results, I developed a capacity to go with the flow without any restrictions and without a need for all the rules and the disciplines that I had followed initially. With my new understanding I enjoy everything I can, including being with friends, traveling, and dedicating myself to charitable organizations or some form of social service where I can make a difference. In the past I have traveled to Nigeria to visit orphanages where basic needs, such as clothing, food, and medical supplies are not available. My focus has always been to address most of the rudimentary needs of people, because if these essentials are not taken care of, a detrimental cycle ensues.

Similarly, my annual travels to India are now primarily dedicated to this mission. The majority of the selfless services or charity organizations with which I am involved now are through an established channel that Amma Karunamayi created, and only a few are ones that I found on my own. I have organized and supported orphanages and food drives for thousands of children, in villages across Southern India, who never before had a substantial meal. As far as I can, I make sure all their needs are met, including school clothing or supplies. At last I can say that I am actively participating in things I really enjoy and can take full advantage of creation to the best of my ability. It feels as though everything is being orchestrated perfectly.

Comments about one's charitable work can easily come off sounding self-congratulatory, but the simple fact is that at this stage one has no choice but to give without expectation of any return. When I see aid workers and others I've met who devote their entire lives to helping the disadvantaged, my contributions seem slight by comparison. And when I look at the lives of teachers like Amma, I'm completely overwhelmed by their full-time commitment to helping others along the spiritual path with little regard for their own time and comfort. Likewise, reaching a higher state of consciousness or attaining realization should not be approached with arrogance or the expectation of gaining something that no one else has. However, this may happen in some cases, in which the journey of realization has not been completed totally or has been interrupted along the way. Unless the journey is complete, fully awakened and experienced oneness it is susceptible to being used by our old inflated ego and we will end up acting like jerks or monsters. It's unlikely that an occasional glimpse of a nondual state or a fleeting transcendental experience will make one fully realized. This is why we must experience samadhi repeatedly, so that we become permanently established in the state of oneness.

FIFTEEN
Conclusions

My new life has brought so much that I am thankful for that I can't begin to describe it all. I have unbounded gratitude to the Supreme Power for bringing me to the ultimate reality: *home at last.* I feel both humbled and relieved that after nine long years this journey has finally come to an end—although I realize that even this end is only temporary. At the same time I often feel exhausted, as if it is time to go home permanently. But this is not in our control, as the dance must continue until it is finished.

I see now that there was always a purpose and a definite goal for everything that happened throughout my life. Meditation, awakening, kundalini's ascending, and Self-realization each played a role, although I had never heard these terms or had any understanding of them as I was growing up. I probably would have never attempted to pursue any of it if I had known the scope of the task that was involved and the toll it would take on me (not that I had any control over this).

According to the Upanishads, once we attain realization or liberation, we continue to live in this embodied life until we complete our remaining predestined life span and our fruit-yielding actions are exhausted. Each of us comes with a particular life span, and realized individuals no longer carry any previous karma nor create new karma. We simply continue to live in the body we are currently in until we reach the end of our life span. It cannot be avoided or changed, but is only reaped or exhausted by being experienced. In other words, even after realization one must complete what is pending, and so this embodied life continues until all the actions or tasks are finished.

Once I realized that I had fulfilled my life's purpose, an idle curiosity imposed itself on my mind as to how long I have to continue before giving up this body. Wondering about this, and to thank my teacher immensely for all the guidance she had given me throughout my journey, I went to see Amma. I felt there was no one better with whom to have this kind of consultation, as she had guided me along my path for some years and I had developed a close attachment to her. I was used to discussing all manner of issues with her and often bombarded her with questions regarding books I had read and other issues that came up during my journey. She was always patient with me and knew exactly what was on my mind. As she had been closely observing the progress of my subtle energy movement, she could tell exactly where I was in my journey and how long it would be before I reached the final destination.

And so, I decided to ask her point blank when I was going to give up the body, to which she responded with a big smile. "You still have so much more to do with this life," Amma said. "How can you go? People like you are needed to do good in the world." She also revealed that, once we are enlightened, we have the capacity of knowing when we can leave the body, and implied that when the time was right, I would know. It made me feel good to believe I would have foreknowledge of my own departure! I also understood what she meant about still having much to do. Since Self-realization enhances our ability to have a positive impact in this world, we become more effective at helping others and contributing wholeheartedly, so why leave when we're at our peak?

What she said also reinforced my belief in destiny due to karma, which could be the reason all the events I've described in this book unfolded as they did. We all will be led to the work we are supposed to do in our life. It doesn't matter who or where we are, the evolution of individual consciousness will take place in all of us when it's time.

As Sri Aurobindo says, "The connectedness to the Source becomes our final destination of life. Our sole purpose in this terrestrial existence is to know the Truth and get in touch with our inner self to become a perfect conscious Being at the end of evolution [through our many lifetimes]. Our life on this earth is a symbolic and concentrated representation of the purpose of the entire universe, which is the evolution of consciousness."[1]

I'm grateful that after many years of inner struggle, I am finally able to experience overwhelming freedom and peace. But I have realized that in the end what matters is how well we run our life with a different approach and motivation. My life feels different now that there is no longer anything to "get" from the world. With this new mental capacity I am able to withdraw from ordinary activities and aim for something extraordinary and more satisfying and fulfilling. I continue to live without any objectives or goals, which seem to have been lost anyway. In a way, there is really nothing to look forward to or anything I really "want" any longer.

Human life is a major spiritual opportunity for consciousness to evolve and for all of us to attain Self-realization, which is an expression of the gift that the Divine offers to those who are ready. Yet our ultimate purpose is not only freeing ourselves from our counterproductive emotions and all the predispositions that get established in our mind from many existences, but also to give meaning to our mundane life. Once we experience our true nature, everything we have been struggling for all along, including power, wealth, praise, knowledge, and recognition, become insignificant. Our aim is not to run after these ego enhancements, but to discover the bliss of how we can most effectively benefit others. This knowledge comes to us only after enlightenment. The ultimate proof lies in our increased interest in becoming involved in activities that serve others. Everything makes perfect sense only after returning to the Source from which we all derive.

After reaching the goal of realization, I contemplated several other questions. Is there more? How far can one go toward the the full magnanimity of Absolute? How many more gradations are there, or is this the ending? This line of inquiry was one of the reasons I continued with my deep meditations. But in time I came to realize there is no such thing as an "ending." Life is an ongoing process, even after higher consciousness becomes permanent. For one thing, this new understanding has to permeate our everyday consciousness and be stabilized. Once the Self is integrated, the rest of our life flows with a kind of inner harmony that makes us feel complete and content. This is not something we need to work at. It happens automatically as we continue with our life in what is called in Vedic Sanskrit terminology the *sahaja samadhi* state. This means to be in our original natural and effortless state of being, remaining permanently in the primal state in which communion with our higher consciousness is continuous. Here the mind is totally free from all doubts, difficulties, and possibilities. We are sure of the Truth because we feel the presence of the Real continuously.

Ramana Maharshi explained the distinctions among the different levels of samadhi as well as anyone I have read. "Holding on to the supreme state is samadhi," he said. "When it is with effort due to mental disturbances, it is savikalpa. When these disturbances are absent, it is nirvikalpa. Remaining permanently in the primal state without effort is sahaja."[2]

And this last was the state I found myself in. Another Indian teacher used a metaphor I find fitting:

> Samadhi is like a big building with many floors. When one is in sahaja samadhi, he is the owner of the whole building. He has the height of nirvikalpa, and the heights far above that, and at the same time he has achieved the perfection, wealth and capacity of all the other floors.
>
> Sri Chinmoy[3]

In earlier chapters I talked about seeing the presence of the Divine everywhere, and feeling it even when I was continuously involved with daily tasks. At this stage of sahaja, I no longer felt the need to do meditation as before, since we are always in that state where we live in the Self as the Self, unattached to all activities and their results. This does not mean that we look different or act differently, but only that we live with our inner self. We function naturally with our day-to-day activities and other tasks just as any other individual. The only difference is that we know what is real and what is not. We may still occasionally enjoy what are commonly known as "the good things in life" or sense pleasures, whether that means going out with friends for dinner and a glass of wine or indulging in sweets. The difference is that we do these things without being attached to them, completely aware that they are just gross obsessions and are not real.

Stories are sometimes told about gurus asking their disciples to refrain from sexual activity while striving for Self-realization. But that is only while *on* the path, when it is important to conserve our vital pranic energy so it can be utilized to elevate our Self toward the final goal. It may be for a matter of months or even a few years or more, but once you attain Self-realization it makes less difference what you indulge in, as everything you do has little impact. Indulging in sense pleasures is not to be considered anything bad, so long as you do not harm others.

Much the same is true of meditation, which is absolutely necessary to achieve Self-realization. But once that point has been reached, it's a matter of individual preference. My curiosity about how much further we can go made me continue with my deep meditations even after realization. With continuous practice the duration of the gap between thoughts increases and we gain the capacity to be absorbed in the Absolute with ease, for much longer. Each level of deepening that took place led me to believe that a further unfolding was going on, but in reality it was just a matter of stabilizing what was already there. The Truth remains the Truth, even though it feels like we are being taken to deeper stages. As these apparently deeper experiences become steadfast, we learn to live with that higher energy field and continue moving forward. Meditation and being with our true nature become part of this existence. But how far we can go or how many different gradations of realized states we can experience, I really can't say. Perhaps there are numerous grades of experience for each person's realization, depending on many factors. Every state and experience varies with each individual and is probably based on some combination of one's karmic predisposition and divine will.

I do know, however, that realization leaves us all with a sense of finally being at home, something I have felt deeply. This feeling is a conscious, undisturbed absorption in the inner Divinity I've been calling the Self. The depth of realization is relative and proportional to one's capacity to attain it. The experience may differ according to temperament and the intensity of one's faith and devotion. As Ramana Maharshi says, "There are grades of experience for the individual but not of reality."[4]

Filled with the knowledge that I was finally home, I went to see my guru once more. During our conversation she declared that my inner journey had been completed, at which I felt great relief. The journey's end had been proven to me through the signs of continual contentment and peace that I express in everything I do, but it was still comforting to hear my guru confirm that.

I had come to understand that Self-realization is not for everyone; the impact is so forceful that those who lack the necessary physical stamina and mental health cannot bear it until it is their time. But I also believe that meditation, yoga, breath control, and other practices can help everyone lead a healthy life. That is one reason I've provided brief guidelines along the way, to help those who may never have tried these spiritual practices and are curious about them get started. Since the purpose of life is to reach Self-realization and know Truth, any effort and preparation toward that end will definitely lead us to a higher level of evolutionary growth.

What the Buddha, Jesus Christ, Yogananda, Ramana Maharshi, and many great souls have realized over the centuries is available to us if we are ready, because the Truth is the same for everyone. Those great masters did not teach their followers to worship them as special personalities, but rather to encounter what they experienced in reaching oneness with God.

Ultimately, I feel that the evolution of consciousness is not something to be proud of or feel superior about. It simply means that we can finally live our life from that higher level of understanding and knowing, with a much greater capacity. "The completion of Self-realization is to be," says Adyashanti, "which means to act, do, and express what you realize."[5] And that is how we continue to function in our day-to-day existence after reaching enlightenment.

Finally, we are nothing more than the formless essence of divinity radiating out, through form itself, that pure primordial energy that some call the Void. As J. Krishnamurti says:

> Energy is action and movement. All action is movement and all action is energy. All desire is energy. All feeling is energy. All thought is energy. All living is energy. All life is energy. If that energy is allowed to flow without any contradiction, without any friction, without any conflict, then that energy is boundless, endless. When there is no friction there are no frontiers to energy. It is friction which gives energy limitations. So, having once seen this, why is it that the human being always brings friction into energy? Why does he create friction in this movement which we call life? Is pure energy, energy without limitations just an idea to him?[6]

Once we experience true peace, then it is no longer a temporary gain but is ours to keep until we give up the gross body. The American Buddhist teacher Jack Kornfield puts it this way: "We know that our true reality is beyond body and mind, and yet because we also live within this limited body and mind, the ordinary patterns of life continue."[7]

Did you ever eat the innermost layer of an onion? I've always felt it has an exceptional taste, but first we must peel off all the exterior layers covering it. Each of us is like an onion with many layers to peel away before we discover our True Self in all its evolutionary perfection. I believe we all incarnate with a purpose and a unique destiny, and that connectedness to Source becomes our final destination through our many lifetimes.

In the end we don't belong to anyone and no one belongs to us, but we all belong to that ultimate Source. Every day we are all playing out our parts and gaining experience so we can evolve. Eventually we all go home to our real home, either by death or by realizing our true nature while still living.

Now that I am *home at last*, I don't mind playing my part. In reality this is what we all do. The play does not change, but we perform our part with much higher capacity after attaining the knowledge of Truth.

So why not enjoy and participate thoroughly in this cosmic drama of the Supreme?

As Nisargadatta Maharaj has said, "It is not the individual which has consciousness; it is the consciousness which assumes innumerable forms in order to manifest."[8]

AFTERWORD
My Early Life

Because my goal in writing this book was to describe as accurately as possible the various stages of the experience of Self-realization, I needed to talk about myself much more than I would like. This is especially ironic because one of the effects of realization is to diminish the ego and expand one's compassion and desire to be of service to others. Yet I have also tried to emphasize the fact that this kind of intensive spiritual transformation can happen to people from ordinary backgrounds with no prior training or exposure to spiritual practice at an early age.

Although I was born in India, a country that has long been associated with ancient spiritual traditions and mystical practices, I was never involved in any particular spiritual tradition as I was growing up. My father worked in the field of entomology at the Indian Agricultural Research Institute in New Delhi, and his goal was to get an advanced degree from an American university. He set out on his own to establish himself in the American Midwest, but despite his best intentions, it was a long time before the rest of the family was able to join him. By the time I arrived in the States, I was almost fourteen, and I was filled with confusion and discomfort at my new surroundings.

I was not fascinated by the Western world as some people are who experience thrills or excitement the moment they land in United States for the first time. This may have been because I was still young and had never traveled far from where I was born and raised until then. From the minute I landed, walking toward the exit door, my eyes were constantly searching for my parents, especially my mother. I had missed her so much in the two years she had been away. I believe in fate and that I am in America today because of her. She wanted all her children to be together, and her perseverance brought me here to join the rest of the family.

I was accustomed to my routines in India and did not want my comfort zone to be disturbed. However, this was not a decision over which I had any control. Because I had lived so many formative years in India, my Eastern cultural roots and ideals had been well developed before I came West. My way of thinking and my likes and dislikes were firmly in place by then. I came to believe that it's more important to maintain strong moral and ethical virtues, as they lead us toward higher consciousness and spiritual growth. I always felt culture is as much a way of life as a view of life. One's way of life doesn't change unless it is inspired by something totally new and different. Our character is built upon a clear vision of our fundamental values that define who we are. How we succeed in life depends solely on the amount of transformation we bring to our character and behavior. This is a matter of balancing our own ideals with the best we draw from, wherever we live.

As a rule I have always been contented with who I am, but finding myself in a new country at the age of fourteen was a culture shock. I disliked many things about my new home and had difficulty adjusting to the new environment, especially the educational system. My father had achieved his goal and earned his PhD, but the only place he could get a teaching position was at a college in Ashland, Wisconsin, a small town near the Canadian border. The winters there were colder and harsher than anything I had ever experienced in the lush tropical climate of India. I hated the long winter months in Ashland with temperatures that often dropped below zero. Hibernating indoors and not seeing the sun shine for days or weeks at a time was depressing, especially for someone from a tropical climate. I also had to adjust to the fact that, as residents of a conservative Midwestern town, the people there had not been exposed to many foreigners. My family and I were probably the first visitors of Indian origin that Ashland had ever seen.

In the beginning I was convinced that our stay in the United States was only temporary and that my family and I would be returning to India soon enough. As the years went by, though, it dawned on me that my family had no intention of ever going back, other than for an occasional visit. As that awareness sank in, I did my best to adjust to the new culture. I finished high school while living with my family and later attended the college where my father was teaching. Tuition was free for family of the faculty, and this allowed my father to put his four children through college.

As time passed, I was able to make good friends at college and was liked by many of my professors. I enjoyed most of the courses I was taking and learned how to handle the academic work well. On the whole I enjoyed my college years far better than high school. My thinking process also changed over the course of time. After being in Western culture for enough years, I observed many differences between East and West in the way the two cultures thought and approached life in general. The Western spirit fascinated me with its penchant for setting and accomplishing goals using one's own power and potentiality. Americans seemed to depend on themselves and to be independent-minded more than many people in India. To some extent the people I encountered followed custom and tradition, but not on as profound a level as the people I had known in India. Most young people in India live at home until they marry and start their own families. By contrast, Americans were true go-getters and genuinely seemed to believe anything was possible. You could be born in poverty and grow up to be president; you could also start your own business and make your fortune by dint of hard work and initiative. All those concepts that may sound like clichés to people raised in this country were quite foreign to someone who had grown up in such a different culture.

After graduating from college in Ashland, I was drawn toward health sciences and decided to pursue a career in that area. I had to leave my home in order to attend a one- year internship program to become a board-certified medical technologist at an accredited hospital in Minneapolis, and that's when life began to look up. Minneapolis was a more cosmopolitan place than Ashland, and I found it easier to fit in and develop a more active social life. I was also excited that I could complete my study quickly and get a job right away, unlike in other fields where many years of schooling are required to earn a position of your choice with a decent salary. The thought of getting a job and my own paycheck excited me tremendously. For the first time since coming to America I was genuinely happy, not so much for the money as for having a job and being independent—a typically American way of thinking!

In all this I had very little help from my parents, who did not provide much guidance or encouragement. Focused on their own survival and becoming acclimated to the new world in which they found themselves, they hadn't worked out a course of action for their children. So I had to figure out things on my own and pretty much plan my own future. This suited me fine because I had always had a clear understanding of my personal preferences and felt comfortable deciding everything on my own. And like most people I wanted to make a good living and be comfortable in whatever position I held.

After finishing my studies I got married and moved to the East Coast. I thanked God for rescuing me from those horribly gloomy Midwestern winters that I had endured for so long. I continued my education, specializing so that I could climb the ladder to higher positions in the field of immunohematology—more commonly known as blood banking, a field of laboratory medicine that deals with preparing blood and its components for transfusion. This required more studying and taking more Board exams. After completing all that, I reached out for other career opportunities that allowed me to work in a variety of pharmaceutical companies and other medical industries. For whatever reason, I never had any problem finding positions to my liking. Call it luck or a blessing from the Divine, but the work I wanted was always there for me. However, I was never really interested in continuously building my career or taking it to higher levels. I was happy doing what

I was doing and excelling in everything while making a good salary.

By this point my husband and I were financially stable, raising our daughters and traveling extensively for my husband's career. His work frequently took him overseas to Costa Rica, Venezuela, Nigeria, and other countries, and I faced my share of challenges putting two daughters through school in a constantly changing environment, but nothing that I could not handle. By and large I was happy and satisfied with whatever life brought about.

After a few years had passed, however, I began to feel that something was missing and began to pursue a spiritual quest while still maintaining a comfortable family life. Though I was content with day-to-day life and on the surface I appeared to be functioning all right, a feeling of dissatisfaction was growing within me. I felt deep down in my consciousness that I needed to do something more, but I couldn't identify exactly what that might be. At times I felt that something was waiting for me, like a figure glimpsed dimly in the dark, but I couldn't make it out. Although I couldn't identify this yearning for something more, I did notice that it was not allowing me to do other things with ease. Most people usually learn to ignore such deep-seated but unidentifiable longings and move on with life as it is. But I wanted to find out what was waiting for me.

And so for many years I went on feeling the void despite the fact that I had everything material that I thought I needed. Was I looking for more money, higher education, recognition, or another career? I was never unduly attracted to the fame, fortune, power, status, or possessions that most people seem to crave, because I believe that the more we have the more we become servants to our possessions. We grow preoccupied with having too many things and our energy and thoughts are constantly devoted to acquiring and taking care of them, leaving no time for Self-development. Having wealth is fine, but how we use that wealth is what makes the biggest difference in our life. As the saying goes, it's all right to *possess wealth but not get possessed by wealth*. Wealth can be a blessing, provided we use it to perform selfless deeds rather than succumbing to greed, egotism, and the kind of mental imbalance that can destroy our character. As many teachers have said, "Joy is not found in sense objects and wealth." I completely abide by such thinking, as I never measured my state of happiness by the amount of wealth I might possess.

In time my husband's career and his extensive international traveling schedule caused me to give up working. I always put his needs and wants before my own concerns for career advancement, and I chose to accompany him on every trip, feeling that it was the right thing to do at that time. At one point when we were living in Nigeria, however, he had a severe heart attack, and because he couldn't get the proper medical care he needed there we moved back to the United States. In the process of adjusting to my husband's health issues, I came to believe that there had to be something that would help him heal faster than the conventional route of Western medicine. I began to learn all I could about holistic methods and other approaches to healing that were more spiritual. I had never considered myself a spiritual person until that time, as my family did not actively practice any particular religion. And yet I had always believed in the existence of a Supreme Power that operates throughout all creation. Now I began to wonder if there might be some connection between these alternative methods and my sense of a Supreme Power in the universe.

And so began in earnest the search for a higher consciousness that I have described in this book, a work I hope will be of some use to my readers. Everything that I have put into it in the course of almost two years was orchestrated by my inner being, which has allowed me to complete the book with such confidence. In the beginning I was apprehensive about how to express everything I had experienced in language that would capture its essence yet be accessible to most readers. But once I got going, it flowed as if someone were directing and coaching me all along the way. I became merely an instrument that wrote what was experienced, in words written by *That,* the divinity within, through my hand. I could not have written such a book without having experienced it all. Everything was generated or revealed sequentially from within, either while I was meditating or while I was focusing on nothing in particular. At certain moments the ideas seemed to pop into my mind, and I quickly put them on paper so they would not be lost.

I also believe that the insight one gains through realization should be shared with everyone. That belief has been the driving force behind my desire to write this book and send it out to the world.

Endnotes

INTRODUCTION

1. Fred H. Meyer, MD, *Don't Give Up Until You Do: From Mindfulness to Realization on the Buddhist Path* (Woodbury, MN: Llewellyn, 2012), p. 3.

CHAPTER 3

1. David Hawkins, *Transcending the Levels of Consciousness* (W. Sedona, AZ: Veritas, 2006) pp. 327-328.
2. Swami Abhedananda et al., *Question of Freedom* (Bombay, India: Central Chinmaya Mission, 1990), p. 56.
3. Donna Lee Steele, "The Soul's Evolutionary Journey: Fate versus Free Will," http://thresholdconsulting.wordpress.com/2011/10/, retrieved Aug. 2, 2014

CHAPTER 4

1. Paramahansa Yogananda, *Man's Eternal Quest: Collected Talks and Essays, Vol. 1* (Los Angeles: Self-Realization Fellowship, 1982) p. 473.
2. Paramahansa Yogananda, *Journey to Self-Realization* (Los Angeles: Self-Realization Fellowship, 1997), p. 312.
3. David Frawley, *Yoga and the Sacred Fire: Self-Realization and Planetary Transformation* (Twin Lakes, WI: Lotus Press, 2005), p 237.

CHAPTER 5

1. Swami Muktananda, *Play of Consciousness* (South Fallsburg, NY: SYDA Foundation, 1978).
2. Jon Kabat-Zinn, *Full Catastrophe Living: Using the Wisdom of Your Body and Mind to Face Stress, Pain, and Illness* (New York: Bantam, 2013).

CHAPTER 6

1. Paramahansa Yogananda, *Journey to Self-Realization: Collected Talks and Essays. Vol. 3* (Los Angeles: Self-Realization Fellowship, 1997), p.431
2. Gopi Krishna, *Living with Kundalini: The Autobiography of Gopi Krishna.* (Boston: Shambhala, 1993), p. 197.
3. Ken Wilber, *The Spectrum of Consciousness* (Wheaton, Ill.: Quest Books, 1993), in the Foreword by John White, p. x.
4. Eckhart Tolle, *The Power of Now: A Guide to Spiritual Enlightenment* (Novato, CA: New World Library, 2004), p. 211.
5. Muktananda, *Play of Consciousness*, p. xi.

CHAPTER 7

1. Paramahansa Yogananda, Journey to Self-realization: Collected Talks and Essays. Vol. 3, (Los Angeles: Self-Realization Fellowship, 1997), p.xxii

CHAPTER 8

1. Jack Kornfield, *After the Ecstasy, the Laundry: How the Heart Grows Wise on the Spiritual Path* (New York: Bantam, 2001), p. 178.
2. B.K.S. Iyengar, *Astadala Yogamala: Collected Works, Vol. 1* (New Delhi, India: Allied Publishers, 2010), p. 76.
3. The Mother, *Commentaries on the Divine Life: Two of the Last Chapters* (Pondicherry, India: Sri Aurobindo Press, 1994), p. 140
4. Mohandas Karamchand Gandhi, *Young India*, Jan. 27, 1927.

CHAPTER 9

1. Claire Hoffman, "David Lynch Is Back . . . as a Guru of Transcendental Meditation," *New York Times Magazine*, Feb. 24, 2013. http://www.nytimes.com/2013/02/24/magazine/david-lynch-transcendental-meditation.html?pagewanted=all&_r=0
2. Hawkins, *Transcending the Levels of Consciousness*, p. 303.
3. Nisargadatta Maharaj, *I AM THAT: Talks with Sri Nsargadatta Maharaj* (Durham, NC: Acorn Press, 1973), p. 272.

4. Swami Muktananda, *Kundalini: The Secret of Life* (South Fallsburg, NY: SYDA Foundation, 1979), p. 36.
5. Yogananda, *Second Coming of Christ: The Resurrection of the Christ Within You, Vol. 1* (Los Angeles: Self-Realization Fellowship, 2004), p. 37.
6. Quoted in Swami Adiswarananda, *Spiritual Quest And The Way Of Yoga*, p. 82.
7. *Ibid.*, p. 82.
8. Quoted in Hawkins, *Transcending the Levels of Consciousness*, p. 253.
9. Swami Nikhilananda, trans., *Selections from the Gospel of Sri Ramakrishna: Annotated & Explained* (Woodstock, VT: SkyLight Paths, 2002), p .96.

CHAPTER 10

1. Muktananda, *Kundalini: The Secret of Life*, 1979, p. 6.
2. Quoted in The Mother, *Commentaries on the Divine Life*, p. 4.
3. Muktananda, *Kundalini: The Secret of Life*, p. 6.
4. Ajit Mookerjee, *Kundalini: The Arousal of the Inner Energy* (Rochester, VT: Destiny Books, 1981), p. 9.

CHAPTER 11

1. Krishna, *Living with Kundalini* , p. 236.
2. The Mother, *Commentaries on the Divine Life*, p. 140.
3. For more detailed information on the phenomenon of misdiagnosis, see Lee Sannella, *The Kundalini Experience* (Lower Lake, CA: Integral Publishing, 1987; first published 1976).

CHAPTER 12

1. David Godman, ed., *Be As You Are: The Teachings of Sri Ramana Maharshi* (New York: Penguin, 1989), p. 137.
2. Quoted in *Autobiography of a Yogi*, p. 148.

CHAPTER 13

1. *Dr. M. W. Lewis: The Life Story of One of the Earliest American Disciples of Paramahansa Yogananda* (Los Angeles: SRF Fellowship, 1960).
2. Godman, *Be As You Are*, p.134.
3. The Mother, *Commentaries on the Divine Life*, p.144.
4. Nisargadatta Maharaj, 1973, p.272.
5. The Dalai Lama, *Becoming Enlightened* (New York: Atria, 2009), p.142.

CHAPTER 14

1. The Dalai Lama, *Parabola,* Vol. 39:1, Spring 2014, p. 156.
2. Quoted in Louis Fischer (ed.), *The Essential Gandhi: An Anthology of His Writings on His Life, Work, and Ideas* (New York: Vintage, 2002).

CHAPTER 15

1. The Mother, *Commentaries on the Divine Life*, p. 4-5.
2. "Spiritual Masters Guide: Ramana Maharshi on Samadhi," http://spiritualmastersguide.blogspot.com/2011/08/ramana-maharshi-on-samadhi.html, retrieved Aug. 9, 2014.
3. Sri Chinmoy, "The Summits of God-Life: Samadhi and Siddhi," *http://www.srichinmoylibrary.com/summits-of-god-life-samadhi-and-siddhi/if-a-master-is-in-sahaja-samadhi-all-the-time-which-is-the*
4. Godman, *Be As You Are*, p. 147.
5. Adyashanti, *Emptiness Dancing*, (Boulder, CO: Sounds True, 2006), p. 1.
6. J. Krishnamurti, quoted in Danielle Föllmi and Olivier Föllmi, *Indian Wisdom: 365 Days*, (London, UK: Thames & Hudson Ltd.).
7. Kornfield, *After the Ecstasy, the Laundry*, p. 121.
8. Jean Dunn, ed., *Prior to Consciousness: Talks with Sri Nisargadatta Maharaj* (Durham, NC: Acorn, 1990), p 26.

Bibliography

Abhedananda, Swami, et al. *Question of Freedom.* Bombay, India: Central Chinmaya Mission, 1990.

Adyashanti. *Emptiness Dancing*. Boulder, CO: Sounds True, 2006.

Dalai Lama, H.H. The. *Stages of Meditation.* Ithaca, NY: Snow Lion, 2003.

———. *Becoming Enlightened*. New York: Atria, 2009.

Dr. M. W. Lewis: The Life Story of One of the Earliest American Disciples of Paramahansa Yogananda. Los Angeles: Self-Realization Fellowship, 1960.

Dunn, Jean, ed. *Prior to Consciousness: Talks with Sri Nisargadatta Maharaj.* Durham, NC: Acorn, 1990.

Fischer, Louis (ed.). *The Essential Gandhi: An Anthology of His Writings on His Life, Work, and Ideas*. New York: Vintage, 2002.

Frawley, David. *Yoga and the Sacred Fire: Self-Realization and Planetary Transformation.* Twin Lakes, WI: Lotus Press, 2005.

Gandhi, Mohandas Karamchand. *Young India*, Jan. 27, 1927.

Godman, David, ed., *Be As You Are: The Teachings of Sri Ramana Maharshi.* New York: Penguin, 1989.

Grof, Stanislav, MD and Christina Grof, eds. *Spiritual Emergency: When Personal Transformation Becomes a Crisis (New Consciousness Readers).* New York: Tarcher, 1989.

Hawkins, David R, MD, PhD. *Transcending the Levels of Consciousness: The Stairway to Enlightenment*. W. Sedona, AZ: Veritas, 2006.

Iyengar, B.K.S. *Astadala Yogamala: Collected Works.* New Delhi, India: Allied Publishers, 2010.

Kornfield, Jack. *After the Ecstasy, the Laundry: How the Heart Grows Wise on the Spiritual Path.* New York: Bantam, 2001.

Krishna, Gopi. *Living with Kundalini: The Autobiography of Gopi Krishna.* Boston: Shambhala, 1993

Maharaj, Nisargadatta. *I AM THAT: Talks with Sri Nsargadatta Maharaj.* Translated by Maurice Frydman. Durham, NC: Acorn Press, 1973.

Meyer, Fred H., MD. *Don't Give Up Until You Do: From Mindfulness to Realization on the Buddhist Path.* Woodbury, Minn.: Llewellyn, 2012.

Mookerjee, Ajit. *Kundalini: The Arousal of the Inner Energy.* Rochester, VT: Destiny Books, 1981.

The Mother (Mirra Alfassa), *Commentaries on "The Life Divine": Two of the Last Chapters.* Pondicherry, India: Sri Aurobindo Press, 1994.

Muktananda, Swami. *Play of Consciousness.* South Fallsburg, NY: SYDA Foundation, 1978.

———. *Kundalini: The Secret of Life.* South Fallsburg, NY: SYDA Foundation, 1979.

Nikhilananda, Swami, trans. *Selections from the Gospel of Sri Ramakrishna: Annotated & Explained.* Woodstock, VT: SkyLight Paths, 2002.

Sannella, Lee. *The Kundalini Experience.* Lower Lake, CA: Integral Publishing, 1987 (first published 1976).

Tolle, Eckhart. *The Power of Now: A Guide to Spiritual Enlightenment.* Novato, CA: New World Library, 2004.

Wilber, Ken. *The Spectrum of Consciousness.* Wheaton, IL: Quest Books, 1993.

Yogananda, Paramahansa. *Autobiography of a Yogi.* Los Angeles: Self-Realization Fellowship, 1998 (first published 1946).

———. *Man's Eternal Quest: Collected Talks and Essays, Vol. 1.* Los Angeles: Self-Realization Fellowship, 1982.

———. *Man's Eternal Quest: Collected Talks and Essays,* Vol. 3. Los Angeles: Self-Realization Fellowship, 1982.

———. *Second Coming of Christ: The Resurrection of the Christ Within You, Vol.* 1. Los Angeles: Self-Realization Fellowship, 2004.

———. *Journey to Self-Realization: Collected Talks and Essays. Vol. 3.* Los Angeles: Self-Realization Fellowship, 1997.

The Yoga Sutras of Patanjali. Translation and Commentary by Swami Satchidananda. Buckingham, VA: Integral Yoga Publications, 2012 (originally published 1973).